JONAH LOMU

By
Kevin Childs

legend books

Published by Legend Books
An imprint of Melbourne Books
4A/178 Collins Street Melbourne Vic 3000, Australia
melbournebooks@hotmail.com

The National Library of Australia Cataloguing-in-Publication entry :

Childs, Kevin.
Jonah Lomu.

ISBN 1 877096 05 9.

1. Lomu, Jonah, 1975 - . 2. Rugby players -
New Zealand -Biography

796.333092

Front cover photo: Nick Wilson
15 July 2000: George Gregan of Australia falls to Jonah Lomu of
New Zealand during the match between Australia and New Zealand
for the Bledisloe Cup at Stadium Australia, Sydney. New Zealand
won 39-35.

To Maureen

Much of this book is drawn from accounts in magazines and newspapers and on websites in New Zealand, Australia, South Africa and Britain. The author wishes to acknowledge the skill and candour of those who write about rugby, and Jonah Lomu, with such insight.

My thanks to James McCausland, a deft copy editor, my brother, Neil, for at least one sin-bin, and those Southland stalwarts, Shaun Yeo and Jimmy Risk, for invaluable archives.

Contents

1

The Untouchables

JONAH LOMU REMEMBERS little about Sunday June 18, 1995, although everyone else who saw or heard what happened has a burning memory. He had been a borderline national selection for the New Zealand All Blacks, missing an early test against Canada as he fought to be fit enough and reach the level of concentration demanded by the selectors for the most searching contest in rugby. It was a warm day at the almost intimate Newlands Rugby Ground, Cape Town. Jonah had not slept. The hulking 20-year-old wolfed down a pile of muffins at breakfast and kept repeating to Zinzan Brooke, a veteran international, "Zinny, I'm an All Black, I'm an All Black."

Jonah lined up on the wing for the All Blacks in the semi-final of the World Cup against England. His performance is considered to be the most remarkable by any person in the history of the game. South Africa ultimately won the tournament and the William Webb Ellis Trophy, but Jonah dominated the event and changed the face of rugby. That day brought to mind another famous victory. In 1924 the University of Notre Dame took on West Point Military Academy at American football. The renowned sports writer Grantland Rice compared a quartet of Notre Dame players to the Four Horsemen of the Apocalypse. Their play, he wrote, so devastated the Army side that they were swept over the precipice. Jonah was to do the same to England.

Jonah had already made an impact in the tournament, scoring twice against Ireland at Ellis Park, Johannesburg. This time the omens on the field were powerful before the kickoff. As Jonah leapt into the air in the climax of the New Zealanders' stirring and challenging haka he caught the eye of opposing winger Tony Underwood. The unfortunate Underwood, giving away 43 kilos to Jonah, claimed later that he wanted to show that he understood and accepted the All Blacks' challenge. So he winked. Right at Jonah. The haka, which historians believe was first used by the original team before a game in New South Wales in 1884, has a proud place in New Zealand lore.

In its climax the team chants:

It is death! It is death!
It is life! It is life!
This is the hairy person
Who caused the sun to shine
Keep abreast! Keep abreast
The rank! Hold fast!
Into the sun that shines

Roused by these words and the war dance, and incensed by what he saw as an insult, Jonah's thoughts were to wipe the wink right off Underwood's face. Coach Laurie Mains had instructed his team: "Give the ball to Jonah," and then see what happens. The pattern was set in five blistering minutes. Andrew Mehrtens, justly celebrated for the flawless nature of his shots at goal, tactical kicking and ability to get his backline moving swiftly, switched directions at the kick-off and England's captain, Will Carling, and Tony Underwood collided under the ball, with Carling knocking it on. The All Blacks won the ball. Within two minutes there was an All Blacks scrum, an All Blacks lineout followed by two rucks won by New Zealand.

Jonah seized an ordinary pass from

fullback Glen Osborne, after it had bounced. Brushing off the unfortunate winker, Underwood, and then stumbling on Carling's utterly desperate tap tackle, he crashed right through fullback Mike Catt to score. "All I remember," says Jonah, "is that I got on the outside, almost tripped, saw Mike Catt and realised I had to run straight into him because I couldn't step." Catt dropped his head and collided with Jonah, who continued on as Catt went to ground as though king-hit. "I couldn't take another step and had to jump," Jonah says of this try "It was bizarre," Catt recalled. Twenty years of practicing tackles meant nothing. "He didn't budge when I hit him, he went over the top of me." On New Zealand television the usually articulate commentator Keith Quinn could only gasp: "Oh, oh, oh" at this mesmeric sight.

Years later the phlegmatic coach Laurie Mains, continues to be astonished by the strength Jonah showed that day. "For a 120 kg player to have that explosive power over 10 metres is devastating," he said. Then there was the Jonah sidestep. At three metres it is double that of most other players.

Carling, relying on videos, stuck out his neck and said that Jonah could be sorted out, no matter how big and strong he was. "The reality was something else," Carling says in his memoirs. "Tony Underwood carried the can for the four tries that afternoon, but Superman on a steamroller would have come off second best." Underwood did get something from that day. He preserved his flattening in an English television advertisement for pizza. Catt, the last line of defence, likes to tell how he received a request from a South African maker of headache cures asking if it could use the footage of him being skittled by Jonah. Presumably Catt was not that interested.

England hooker Brian Moore wrote: "The truth was that you had to rely on existing defensive patterns, on first-time tackling...But Lomu simply battered his way through three tackles and scored. It was not a strategic collapse on our part. There were three players in the cover and he simply ran through all three." At the restart New Zealand won the ball and attacked from within their own 22 after Walter Little broke a tackle. A three-pass exchange hurled Josh Kronfeld over the line and with the conversion it was 12-0. Carling:" After the second score I gathered the team round and told them not to panic... But after the fourth try I was unable to convince myself. New Zealand were touched by genius that day…they were untouchable. It was like 15-year-olds against a men's side." Moore recalled: "These were devastating blows, stunning and bewildering. Any moment you expected to wake up, sweating but safe, in your bed." Says Underwood, "With Jonah switching play they were an awesome team to play against. We never stood a chance."

When it was all over and England had been bundled out Carling described Jonah as an awesome athlete who was fast, dynamic and direct. Unfortunately, Carling also used the term "freak". Like much that was coming out of English rugby at that time, it was wrong and inadequate. Yet this description was to be repeated as high-praise by Jonah's Wellington teammate, the elusive try-getting All Blacks wing turned centre, Tana Umaga. "Jonah is a freak," he says. "He can do things that I will never be able to do. Sometimes at training I watch him. He's awesome. He's bigger than me, he's stronger than me and he's faster than me. There isn't anyone in the world who can do the things he can do."

Jonah humiliated his opposite number at Newlands. He showed the glory of great rugby and its awesome level of toughness, which can spill into violence, but not on this day. The men in the white jerseys bearing the red rose fell or faltered beneath the size 13 boots of the 1.9 metres (6ft 5in), 116 kilos (18 stone) juggernaut. After the match the phones were busy. Kingsley Jones took a call from the owner of the Washington Redskins American football team, who said, "Name your price." In an age when English First Division soccer is full of Frenchmen, when the Australian Socceroos consists of an expatriate foreign legion, and when stars of all sorts of sports blithely swap clubs and even nations while breaking fans' hearts, Jonah stayed loyal. He may have flirted with rugby league and English rugby when he was temporarily dropped from his national side, but he followed through on his declaration that what meant everything was pulling on the black jersey.

Among the hugely impressed 2.5 billion television viewers of this astonishing match was the media tycoon Rupert Murdoch. He phoned his top executive in Australia. Days later Murdoch's News Corporation signed a deal to create Super 12 rugby and the Tri-Nations competition for almost $800 million. It was the end of an amateur sport and the start of a global legend. The boy from South Auckland was about to become the face of world rugby. The story of Lomu is the stuff of national myths. Every element is there: the poor upbringing, the struggle for fame and fortune on the football field, the inevitable setback through a career-threatening illness, then the phoenix-like comeback to reclaim glory and his place as a national hero. Jonah may not have been able to find time yet to accept an offered role as a bad guy in a James Bond film, but so many other aspects of his career smacks of a true-life drama. A management that assiduously cultivates a glowing picture of Jonah jealously guards his every move. The irony is that he is idolized abroad and often scorned at home, reaping profit without honour, perhaps. The Japanese saying that the tallest nail gets the hammer truly applies here and yet the machine called Jonah rolls inexorably onwards.

All nations crave heroes. Some, such as Don Bradman, Muhammed Ali, Babe Ruth and Michael Jordan, have gone beyond the realm of legend and sporting sainthood. The smaller and more remote a country the greater the need for superstars to strut the global stage, to radiate confidence and pride, if not hubris. New Zealand has long enjoyed some phenomenal successes among its sporting stars. Edmund Hillary conquered Everest with Sherpa Tensing, Peter Blake wrested the America's Cup from the United States, and then there are the remarkable horses, from Phar Lap on, who consistently plunder the racetracks of Australia and beyond. In another sphere, Kiri Te Kanawa has enchanted audiences with her wondrous voice.

For almost a century the All Blacks were rarely beaten. Even today, in spite of some remarkable losses, their all-time winning average is an astonishing 72 per cent. In seeking to explain this success and the fervour that surrounds and supports it, Serge Blanco, one of rugby's greatest attacking fullbacks, who was capped 91 times for France in spite of smoking forty cigarettes a day and an aversion to training, conjures up the surreal. New Zealanders, he explained, were the repositories of the whole magic of rugby. "Against them you have pleasure, even when losing, because New Zealanders honour rugby."

Others talk of the mystical if not mythical culture of rugby, an unusual term to cover head-butting, gouging and sometimes a bit of biting among forwards in the scrum, as well as the heart-stopping movements of the ball from half-back along the back line, as player after player whips a pass away just as they are grounded, on to the wing for the sprint to the line. With new rules to rid it of the dull, time-wasting and unattractive elements, the game evolved, as did Jonah. In came professional rugby, played by full-time teams at a high speed pace, with relentless forward movements interspersed with pin-point passing, little chip kicks over defenders followed by slick gathering of the bouncing oval ball and ever-changing back attacks. The Super 12 contest, with its franchised teams and bonus points for tries added some of the quick thrills that one-day matches brought to cricket.

The myth emerges when on the wing is Jonah, his nation's youngest Test cap, soon-to-be the most famous rugby player on earth takes his place. He is an individual who is destined to become a mighty and feared All Black in a land where the player has never been greater than the team.

Jonah Tali Lomu is often described as the most illustrious All Black of modern times. He is doubtless the only player in the world who, on receiving the ball, can make an entire crowd rise to their feet as one. Superlatives, some excessive, all fail in the face of the fierce charges of this son of an impoverished family from Tonga, tell-tale tuft sprouting from an otherwise hairless dome, ball tucked like a child's toy in his left hand, right hand fending off opponents, or those tree trunk legs almost casually running over them. This is one of the compelling images of modern sport. One outcome has been his 34 tries for 170 points in 55 New Zealand test matches, putting him fourth on the table of try-scorers, just below other great wingers, John Kirwan, Christian Cullen and Jeff Wilson. Another is that he has become a metaphor. When Clive James, the expatriate Australian wit, was seeking to describe for newspaper readers events in the British elections in 2001, he reached for Jonah.

To make plain the plight of the Tories, James had already summoned the shades of a pair of Roman consuls as well as that of Montgomery and the Panzer division at Arnhem. When he came to the seat of Cheddar Gorge, where the two main parties were under threat from the Liberal Democrats, Clive needed something powerful. The poll figures for the Lib Dems were on the rise. He saw this result as being just like "a Jonah Lomu run on the wing with a smile of pity for the opposing forwards as they moved across too late."

Beyond his place as a handy metaphor,

Jonah ranks eighth on the list of the most prolific try scorers in rugby history. The highest try-scorer in World Cup history, he is the youngest player to score 10 Test tries and first and the youngest to score 12 Test tries in a calendar year. Not since 1905 had an All Black scored four tries in a Test against England. Jonah did it ninety years later. He began 2002 with 125 points from 25 tries in Super 12. Playing for his third Super 12 team, Wellington Hurricanes, he went on to notch up a half century of games in this competition, which includes appearing for the Auckland Blues when they won the inaugural title. He turned 27 in May 2002, so without injury and any flare up of a crippling kidney condition that sidelined him for a year, his horizons seem boundless.

Jonah does incite remarkable enthusiasm. The London *Times* held that, in terms of his sport, he is Ronaldo and Michael Jordan combined. The effect of his debut in world rugby has been compared to an unseeded Boris Becker winning Wimbledon or Tiger Woods taking the Masters by 15 shots.

His name penetrates the furthest reaches. Mike Tyson was pounding a heavy bag when he took a question from a South African journalist, "Ah, South Africa. That's that Jonah Lomu fella, ain't it?" said big Mike. A discovery by a New Zealand scientist in the field of male growth genes is called the Jonah Lomu effect. This effect was truly demonstrated when the game at which Jonah excels changed forever after he devastated England in South Africa in 1995. On that day he showed how he could destroy the morale of opposing teams. What followed is that, while rugby may be, as one wit described it, a game of boots, brains, balls and bladders, for a media magnate with a craving for a sport with a global pull it was ideal as entertainment for a worldwide television audience.

Sport has been defined as an activity in which almost every moment is a moment of truth, in other words the complete opposite of working in politics. The Jonah Lomu moments of truth are many and at times profound. They show a lot of the deepest qualities of sport, such as pride, beauty, strength, perfection and fallibility. It is about occasions when someone seizes a moment of destiny or manages to exceed limitations.

The sight of Jonah setting off from inside his own half, bumping off five tacklers as he rips along the sideline, is just such a moment. Such moments endure. In New Zealand they have the most potent of memories, for the utter dominance by the black jersey had begun ninety years before the South African epiphany when a New Zealand team revolutionised the game by keeping the ball in hand instead of booting it downfield and chasing it. This passing game annihilated British sides. Shots at goal were forsaken for whipping the ball sideways or crunching through with it.

In 356 games, the All Blacks have now won all but 100, including 16 drawn. Between September 1965 and June 1969, they had a fourteen-game winning streak. In spite of this long reign, however, New Zealand has only once won the World Cup, beating France 29-9 in the final of the inaugural competition, played in Australia and New Zealand in 1987 and now competed for every four years. Jonah Lomu is driven by a craving to hold this trophy, which he would surely have done but for a referee's decision.

Paradoxically, in spite of all this, or perhaps because of it, Jonah attracts fierce criticism at home, perhaps because of the notice he gets abroad. If success is not immediate, fans of his Wellington province call for his head. He consistently attempts to rebut his critics by doing what he does best, scoring tries, but he is noticeably restricted in Super 12 and Tri Nations contests. Jonah complained of frustration in Super 12 during 2002, saying that he was not getting the ball from set phases. "We have rarely seen the ball going out wide and I don't know why that is, it's just happening,' he told the Dominion newspaper in Wellington. "But it is a bit annoying, because I wouldn't mind getting some ball.' Then, as if to answer his earlier query, he said, "I try to get into the game, but the opposition are always cutting me off. They come up and stop the passes and when I do get the ball the centre and wing are on top of me." Perhaps these teams know too well the once angry young man.

2

Man Angry

THEY CALLED IT Man Angry. Jonah and his childhood friends had this nickname for Mangere East, the tough part of South Auckland where they grew up. Jonah, like many who have come from hardened roots, does not talk about it much, but he will sometimes ask an audience to picture him as a poor Polynesian aged 13, spending his time hanging around the streets. A mugger sees him sitting alone on a footpath and demands that he hand over his smart runners. Jonah slowly rises and keeps on rising until he looks down at the thug. "Sorry," mutters the would-be assailant, "I've changed my mind," and whips away.

This is the Auckland of the film *Once Were Warriors*, a city of rival Maori, Samoan and Tongan gangs. Jonah was 12 when his uncle and a cousin were murdered. Jonah also talks about a street called The Gauntlet. A freeway has since obliterated it, but back then, he says, if you could run The Gauntlet you were all right. "You only walked it if you were stupid or had guts. A couple of mates and me decided to walk it when I was about twelve. If you didn't know how to fight, you were in trouble. But I was OK. I could fight and I could run. I got my sports talent from my mother. She used to be a runner, and a lot of my uncles, her brothers, played rugby for Tonga. A couple of them were boxers, too."

Jonah needed this streetwise strength when faced with the acid-penned profile writers of London's fiercely competitive newspapers. The young man, like the boy in Mangere East, slowly rose and kept on rising in their sceptical estimation. Charming, natural and courteous, gushed one writer. Ask him anything and he never flinches. *Your best friend, Danny, was killed in a fight as a teenager?* " Yeah. There was this street fight between a bouncer and these guys. Danny was just taking a short cut home and he walked into it. He got stabbed 27 times in the chest They slashed his face from cheek to cheek, cut his wrists open, cut him open, he was a real close friend." *You saw your uncle killed?* "Yeah, it was when my uncle was decapitated at the shopping centre. It was a bit of violence between two rival Polynesian groups. He was chopped up, basically, with a machete. My parents said, 'Well, that's enough killing. Time for you to leave the area'."

Leaving meant moving south of Auckland at age 14 to board at Wesley College for almost four years He could scarcely have found a better rugby academy. Jonah had already represented Auckland Primary Schools in rugby league. His early sporting ambition was to be a decathlete and he showed his qualifications by shattering records on the athletic track, covering 100 metres in less than 11 seconds. Entering a school athletics competition, he competed in two sprints, a relay, a hurdles race, two throwing competitions, the long jump and the triple jump, winning them all. When he played for Wesley Sevens in 1992 he was awesome. Murray Deaker, a leading sports broadcaster, remembered a day in 1992: "My kids (who were) all about his age were watching him on television and they yelled out that I had to come and watch this abnormal player. I watched Jonah playing that day and he was, in the kindest possible way, a freak."

With a roll of just 300 boys and 80 girls Wesley, which is affiliated with the Methodist Church, opens its doors to students with a Maori or Pacific background. Founded in 1844 near

Pukekohe, Wesley is able to claim the title of the most successful rugby school in the world. Over ten years it has dominated the national schools championship, winning in 1990, 1993, 1997 and 2001. Sometimes its pack has been heavier than the All Blacks. Its Sevens sides have been national champions for the past two years. In 2001 its second XV won the Counties first XV competition and the third XV won the Waikato second XV Cup. The first XV racked up almost 1000 points in an unbeaten season.

To pay for Wesley his parents took out a second mortgage on their home. They have four children younger than Jonah and his father Semisi put in a lot of overtime at his job as a mechanic. Later, when other schools were on the prowl with the offer of scholarships in return for his rugby prowess, Jonah was given a full scholarship at Wesley. Jonah remembers his crucial move this way: "I was really close to everyone [who was] getting killed. I was in trouble. Police trouble. But they couldn't put me in jail because I was too young. I argued for a whole year about school, but then I found out about rugby and the rest is history...

"I started in rugby league and things were going really well, but the problem was that my parents wouldn't let me play on Sundays and the trials were always on Sundays. I had to go to church."

On the field he was short-tempered. If he were hit he would chase that opponent for the rest of the game. In one match the ball had left the ruck when an opposing player struck Jonah across the face. "I looked at him, and my mum, who was there, looked at me, and I just carried on playing. My mum's fear was always that I didn't know my own strength. But after that game she said to me: 'You've done it. You're your own person now, and you can make your own decisions. Trust in the Lord and do what you believe to be right.' I said: 'I want to play on Sundays'."

Switching from league presented problems. Jonah would charge into a union ruck with the ball. At the tackle there was no play-the-ball as in league. Instead, he found himself being rucked. That is, raked with the studs of footy boots as an encouragement to release the ball.

At Wesley College he came under the influence of deputy principal and First XV coach Chris Grinter, who encouraged him to realise his potential. Grinter recalls this hulking 14-year-old who, although playing lock, was as fast as a wing.

Jonah had also been spotted by national selectors, playing for New Zealand under-17s in 1991-92 and was still in the back row when he was picked for New Zealand Secondary Schools in 1992-93. He was the leading try scorer in both these national sides. In the 1993 National Secondary Schools Sevens titles Jonah erupted from his own 22-metre line to score. Even when starting out in union, however, he was never a student of the game.

When chosen for a school rugby union side his first tournament was at Te Kuiti in the North Island of New Zealand. On the way there he heard much about the famous Te Kuiti Club and its massive, magnificent legend, Colin 'Pinetree' Meads, chosen by fans as the greatest All Blacks of all time. "Who's Pinetree?" asked the innocent young Jonah. He listened to the story of the Meads era, and of Pinetree's phenomenal strength and power, including a tale about him carrying sheep under his arms to the top of a hill. "Were the sheep tired?" asked Jonah, the city boy.

From school he moved his pyrotechnical display to the Hong Kong Sevens. Videos show him breaking four tackles to score for that side against England in 1994 in what was almost a precursor of the eruption to come the following year against the same nation. In Hong Kong he burst through the steely Fijians as if they were children. While still at school, he was player of the tournament in the winning New Zealand side. "He just exploded on the scene," says New Zealand's Sevens champion Eric Rush, "and the next two years he was even better."

Rush had become close to Jonah. The tangy flavour of their friendship was caught when Rush recounted his invitation to young Jonah to join The Mongrels, an unofficial Kiwi Sevens side going to the world championships in Singapore.

Rush: Do you want to go to Singapore?

Lomu: Sure. Why not?

Rush: How quick can you pack your bags?

Lomu: When do we go?

Rush: Tomorrow, bro

Lomu: Sweet.

The Mongrels reached the finals, only to lose to the top Sydney club, Randwick.

At Wesley, too, Chris Grinter introduced Jonah to the mentor who would change his life. Phil Kingsley Jones, a knockabout who had represented Wales, was involved in selecting the Counties

Manawatu side when he noticed Jonah at 14 playing in Wesley's back row. Jonah was asked to join a Counties development squad for aspiring youngsters. On leaving school he began a short career as a bank officer with ASB Bank of New Zealand, a job that he says gave him a grasp on the commercial world. He next sought a marketing position, but football intervened. "I never really planned a career in sport and rugby at all," he has said, "it just happened."

His triumph at the Hong Kong Sevens was followed in May 1994 by his first game for Counties at age 18. That shrewd tactician, the then All Blacks coach Laurie Mains, recalls asking Jonah's provincial coach to play him on the wing. In this unfamiliar position Jonah took a pounding from tacklers, but notched up three tries on debut. It was to become harder as he stepped up from Counties to become an All Black at age 19 years and 45 days, only to have to turn out against the tough and wily French on 26 June 1994 after playing just four first class games. He was not ready.

Realising that his size may have meant an inability to turn quickly, a criticism with some basis that will forever be leveled against him, the French chipped the ball over his head; he struggled in New

Zealand's 22-8 loss at Christchurch and then the 23-20 defeat in Auckland. He was soon dropped. He can joke now that not only was he the youngest All Black, but also the youngest former All Black, but his pain was palpable. This blooding may have served to give him resolve for the World Cup the following year, however. Even Mains now admits that maybe too much was asked of Jonah in '94.

John Kirwan, for a decade a try-scoring machine (96 games for New Zealand, including 35 tries in 63 tests) had hammered the young Jonah in the All Blacks trials. Kirwan, only a few centimetres shorter than Jonah, realised what was happening. "You could see the future of the game right there," he later said. Jonah had been moved to the most difficult position on the field – the wing. As Kirwan notes, playing well there requires an innate understanding of angles. When do you decide to come in to take out the opposing fullback? You are at the end of the line. There may be two or three of the opposition coming at you. An instant decision is needed.

After packing the scrum at school, the wing can be the loneliest outpost. There were other problems, as Kirwan dryly acknowledged. "There wasn't a lot of defence for the outside backs in the

All Blacks and Jonah still made some mistakes in that area. But there weren't too many people who wanted to run at him, because when he gets his hands on them, he hurts them."

Kirwan's tactic was to try to crowd Jonah, reducing his angle of attack, giving him an outside break and try to herd him towards the sideline. Or he would simply try to block him with his body. "If you've got courage, you'll put your body on the line and you won't stop him, but you'll slow him enough for someone else to catch him." And so we see those riveting images of Jonah, two or three players hanging off him like life-size Christmas ornaments, yet often off-loading the ball in the face of a reduced defence.

In turn, Jonah explains that he tried to model himself on Kirwan, who in mid 2002 was appointed national coach of Italy, and who starred for the Auckland Warriors at Rugby League while Jonah was setting the world alight. They played together in Jonah's first two tests. Jonah studied other large players, such as Emile N'Tamack of France and Australia's Joe Roff. "While there is no substitute for pace," Jonah says, "there is more [to the position], such as alignments of defence and attack. Wingers also have to keep talking with the inside backs and forwards. You've got to make sure they know where you are.

"I don't think a lot of people understand what's required from a wing on defence and how hard it can be. It doesn't matter how many years you've played on the wing it still remains hard. It's often very much a split-second thing."

Then there are the smaller wings, including France's Christophe Dominic and Phillippe Bernat-Salles, who, said Jonah, can simply outstrip the opposition with pace. "Small guys are so tricky on their feet and are hard to mark. You're never sure how to make a contact tackle on them. They don't stand still for you and there's always a danger of going too high, getting them around the neck and getting yourself ordered off."

Being ordered off was far from Jonah's mind when he faced his next ordeal, a rite of passage in becoming an All Black. In the raw world of Australian politics one leader denigrated an opponent by saying that he lacked ticker. That is, guts. The English like to talk of a person having bottle. Laurie Mains, as All Blacks coach from 1992 to 1995, had his own term. He told Jonah: "If you show me you have got the apple, you'll make it as an All Black."

This was when Jonah was being put through the most severe physical endurance tests, firstly at Owen Delany Stadium, Auckland, in December 1994, then at a three-day training camp during February 1995 in Taupo, on the North Island. It was as if the footballers were being trained for the SAS. Ever the martinet, Mains forced his squad through punishing drills, push-ups and 150-metre sprints beyond number. "Those tests in Taupo," Jonah was to recall, "were to establish who had the apple and who didn't. You just had to finish. I think I crawled across the finishing line a few times, but I got there." At times Jonah was a lap behind the rest.

All Blacks captain Sean Fitzpatrick, rated one of the game's foremost players, worked hard to encourage Jonah during these tough times. When Fitzpatrick dropped back to run with Jonah, the whole team followed suit. They continued into a fourth pre-World Cup camp at Christchurch, where there were still doubts about Jonah's fitness. The irony is that a groin injury to Eric Rush, who had taken young Jonah to the Singapore Sevens, meant a place for Jonah in the World Cup squad.

His tournament began with two tries in the 43-19 win over Ireland at Ellis Park. Wales were dispatched 34-9, with Jonah being replaced. He scored again in Pretoria in the quarterfinal against Scotland, won 48-30. Then came his dazzling performance against England.

3

Jonah Inc.

HAVING DISPOSED OF the English, New Zealand prepared for the 1995 World Cup final against South Africa. A facsimile from young fans clicked out of the team's machine. "Remember," it read, "rugby is a team game. All 14 of you make sure you pass it straight to Jonah." There was to be no reprise of the storming of England, however, and the Springboks got up 15-12. In a memorable scene, South Africa received the cup from its President, Nelson Mandela, who wore the green Springbok jersey once so despised by his people as a symbol of racism. The Republic had the cup, but Jonah, as South African captain, Francois Pienaar observed, "Put the world game up there".

Many New Zealanders still believe that the All Blacks were deliberately poisoned before the final in South Africa. Certainly the All Blacks' hotel arrangements in Johannesburg were chaotic and security was in disarray. Two days before the final an outbreak of diarrhoea and vomiting affected almost all the team and there was talk of trying to delay the final. Coach Mains remains cautious about exactly what happened, confining himself to noting that everybody was ill. Jonah shows his sporting qualities by saying that if a team can be put on the field, then so be it.

Springbok captain Pienaar concerned himself only about tactics. "All we spoke about is James Small on the wing not giving Jonah outside space." Years later the jokes about this day were still circulating. On rugby websites there appeared versions of an exchange when the Springboks were working out their strategy before the final. Coach Kitsch Christie turns to James Small:

"Right, James, tell me how are we going to deal with this guy, Jonah Lomu?"

"Okay, boss, I'm gonna angle my run so I push him towards the touchline and use it as an extra man, just forcing him out for a lineout."

"Okay. But what if he cuts inside you?"

"Well, then I'll angle it so that he's running back towards our cover defence and Joost will be there to help me smother him and bring him down."

"Uh-huh. And what if he comes straight at you?"

"Well, if he runs straight at me I'll get some crap off the ground and throw it in his face, blinding him."

"What? But there won't be any crap on the ground."

"When he's running straight at me boss, yes there will!"

As it turned out, the Springboks did bundle Jonah into touch. They also roughed him up, but Jonah now simply sticks to his line that if he had two players on him that left a hole elsewhere in the defence. There were further significant issues for him in this final, too. Commentators complained that he was cruelly under-used, and had referee Ed Morrison not ruled a marginal pass to Jonah as forward, he would probably have scored to win the cup. Such a decision alone would be enough to keep his ambition on fire for the next World Cup. When time was blown the scores were locked at 9-all. South Africa's World Cup was won by a Joel Stransky dropped goal. It was over and all Jonah wanted to do was to go home.

Pienaar continues to flash a wide smile when he notes that Jonah is yet to score against the Springboks, although he returned the compliment by denying lock Mark Andrews an almost certain try in the All Blacks dour 12-3 won over South Africa at Newlands in the opening Tri-Nations match in July 2001. Jonah and Doug Howlett sliced through the Springboks in the first half of this game, which ended with captain Bobby Skinstad lamenting: "Every time you lose in this jersey it's a tragedy."

A month after the World Cup the New Zealand Rugby Football Union declared that Jonah Lomu was a registered trademark and it had commercial authority over its use. The value of this trademark was soon demonstrated. Many critics rate Jonah's performance in a Bledisloe Cup match in Sydney in 1995 as one of his greatest.

The chronically competitive trans-Tasman rivalry has resulted in some ferocious match-ups and it is not for nothing that New Zealanders flaunt t-shirts proclaiming that they support the All Blacks and any other team playing Australia. Although he only scored once in the 34-23 win, he helped make three other tries in a masterful demonstration of strength, skill and speed.

In July 1996 Jonah again contributed towards an astonishing 43-6 demolition of Australia in Wellington in the first professional match between the two sides. Leg and shoulder injuries had slowed his progress that season, although he did score in the first

Super 12 match, when Auckland took on Natal.

The London *Daily Telegraph* defined the Wellington game as perfection on a rugby pitch. It had rained all week. The notorious wind howled over a boot swallowing bog. Australia had thrashed Wales and Canada and showed their usual confidence. Playing for forty minutes in the teeth of a gale, the All Blacks scored four tries and scarcely made a mistake.

Jonah erupted into midfield from his blind-side, taking his team up field and giving the forwards a target. "Most teams blessed with a Lomu would have launched him all day," wrote the *Telegraph's* Paul Ackford, "but New Zealand did not. They refused to rely on the exploits of one individual, even when that individual was doing all the right things. That, really, is the ultimate tribute."

The pace and skill of New Zealand that day was breathtaking. They scored after 85 seconds. For the first twenty-one minutes they played without an error. And they held on as the Wallabies threw their considerable arsenal at them.

Jonah did have a setback later that season when given a rare week's suspension after a disciplinary panel found him guilty of a 'spear tackle' in a game against Canterbury. Jonah says he rates this as his worst time in the game, although he does say the same about being dropped from the All Blacks. This charge came about after he was accused of a dangerous tackle on Canterbury fullback Kieran Flynn during Counties' 46-33 semi-final win. Flynn was not injured, but the judicial committee held that the tackle was dangerous because of its capacity for serious injury.

Four years later he was again suspended, this time for two weeks, after a similar tackle on Wallaby centre Nathan Grey during a match between the New South Wales Waratahs and the Hurricanes in Sydney. Jonah was sin-binned by South African referee Andrew Watson. On his return to the field, Jonah helped the Hurricanes move ahead 27-3. But his deliberate knock-on just before half time led to him being ordered off for the rest of the game. A three-man judiciary panel decided Watson had been too lenient in the first misdemeanour and imposed the two-week ban. He did not complain, saying it had been "such a split second thing. It was sort of like a bit out of control."

A groin infection seemed likely to sideline Jonah late in 1996, but he recovered to turn out for a keenly awaited appearance for New Zealand Barbarians against England. Surprisingly,

Lawrence Dallaglio and Jason Leonard were able to bring him down early in that match, but when the English tired, Jonah tapped the acceleration, charging into rucks, tying up numbers of the opposition to create gaps. His opposing winger, Jon Sleightholme, giving away considerable height and weight, had talked of relishing the encounter, but in the twenty-fifth minute Jonah plucked a loose ball from his feet and began to run, brushing off Sleightholme with that big right hand. Just under an hour later the performance was repeated.

Before that game Craig Joiner of Scotland received some publicity as the only Briton then to have played opposite Jonah twice. "You've got to get in behind that hand-off," was Joiner's advice. His achievement of reducing Jonah's try count to one lent him some credibility. "But there again, you could almost write a thesis on how to stop that man. You've got to hit him within seconds. You've got to make every pass he receives a hospital pass. When someone is in front of him, he bumps them off. What people don't give him credit for is that he's so good on his feet. You can tap-tackle him, but he will keep his balance."

Every time Jonah was near the ball for the

New Zealand Baabaas there were roars of anticipation. And while it was Carlos Spencer's try that tied up the match for the Baabaas, it was Jonah's ability to attract large opposition numbers when he ran that made the space for Spencer to score. Jonah scored four tries in New Zealand's 30-16 win.

Little seemed to be going well for Jonah as 1999 opened. In January he, Joeli Vidiri and Isitolo Maka were dropped from the All Blacks four-day training camp at an air force base for failing to meet fitness standards. Jonah protested that he was the strongest and fittest he had been at that time in a season and was only a lap off meeting the three-kilometre endurance time laid down by the selectors. He had been in the triumphant Sevens squad, capturing gold medals at the Commonwealth Games, yet there was criticism that he had gone to England for three weeks over summer, where he talked at children's charity functions. In England he had trained in sub-zero temperatures, including running around Hyde Park in London.

By January experts such as the former All Blacks turned scholar, diplomat and commentator, Chris Laidlaw, were asking whether the world had seen the best of Jonah. His life was split between the simplicity of his home and family, the status of a publicly owned sporting superstar of Olympian proportions and as a player contractually bound to deliver results in a gruelling year-round schedule. "It takes a personality of extraordinary maturity and strength of character to do all these things," he wrote in the *New Zealand Herald*. "Jonah, for all his patent sincerity and his obvious desire to do the right thing, is no Michael Jordan." Jonah, he sharply noted, would need more than his undoubted but rarely seen ability to swerve and step than his penchant to imitate a double-decker bus.

By May Jonah's standing had improved to such a degree that he was back in the All Blacks squad for the World Cup, yet Laidlaw was still questioning whether Jonah had overcome his demons of hesitancy, self-doubt and an inability to do what he once did with such spectacular results. He produced an electrifying moment when New Zealand A met France, gathering the ball, swerving, and then powering past two French speedsters to casually dot down between the posts. Laidlaw shrewdly noted Jonah had been asked to do too much. He had been used as a short-range howitzer or a dummy runner up the middle, around lineouts or back near the Number 8 position of his youth. The result was that he often got the ball when he was unprepared or out of position. His great speed was nullified. Opponents who moved the ball quickly down his side of he field had occasionally made him look ponderous and slow-witted.

In July 1999 he came on to replace Umaga in Auckland, where the All Blacks ran over Australia 34-15. This was Jonah's Year of the Substitute. In five successive internationals he came off the bench. This was also to be the year of New Zealand's largest ever defeat, 28-7, at the hands of Australia in August. During the All Blacks' 34-18 win over South Africa, Jonah did not come on until the thirty-fourth minute, this time to replace Daryl Gibson. Jonah drew swag of tacklers, passed to captain Taine Randell, who in turn threw a long pass to Christian Cullen for a game-breaking try. He had survived a lot, but the World Cup was coming up again.

4

French Kiss

TONGA COMPILED 105 videotapes of the All Blacks for their opening game of the World Cup in Bristol, England, in 1999. The English, who were soon to face the All Blacks, knew they were in for sleepless nights as Jonah picked up two simple tries in his first international for more than a year in the 45-9 win, while some of his aunts showed loyalty for homeland over family by barracking loudly from the stands for Tonga.

The All Blacks and Jonah in particular looked set for a glorious World Cup. "Lomu the Magnificent Black Destroyer Back to his Best," boomed the headlines as he helped his side to a 30-16 win over England in their pool match. Rugby writers marveled at his pace and power. "Anybody with a rugby heart will rejoice to see Lomu playing such a part," exulted Stephen Jones in the London *Sunday Times*. "He put rugby on a global sporting map, he has fought his way back through serious illness and there he was yesterday, pulling out a big one at precisely the correct moment."

The *Sunday Express's* commentator noted, "He was frozen out for most of an inspirational and emotional occasion, but in the end Jonah Lomu returned to haunt England with a decisive try in a record All Blacks win at Twickenham." His 55-metre run left white jerseys and red roses trailing. Martin Johnson, the England captain, who honed his skills in New Zealand, acknowledged, "When Lomu scored his try, a fantastic try, it turned the match."

In 1995 it had been Underwood, Carling and Catt who failed to stop the freight train. Jonah screamed for the ball at Twickenham and now Jeremy Guscott was flicked aside, and then Austin Healey tried for Jonah's knees. Dan Luger and Matt Dawson brought him down, but he had grounded the ball on the line. Once again an ominous and enormous shadow loomed over the World Cup. The game was poised at 16-all at the fifty-seventh minute when Jonah bellowed for possession. "I was screaming for the ball at the top of my lungs," Jonah says. "I knew I had some space and had to take this opportunity." His match-saving 60-metre streak to the line synthesized as he screamed at halfback Andrew Mehrtens, "Hit me `Mehrts,' hit me." Mehrtens later quipped: "My long pass made it and all Jonah had to do was beat five tacklers." In came four tacklers. Each was brushed off or crashed through. As Jonah dived over to score, England backrower Lawrence Dallaglio kneed him in the face. Jonah recalls, "I saw three red lights in front of me saying, `Don't hit him or you'll be out of the tournament.' I kept my composure." Dallaglio, formerly captain of England, had been reinstated in the game three months earlier after being suspended when a newspaper reported that he had admitted taking drugs. He later said that he had just been boasting and telling white lies. Now a melee broke out as the referee called for calm. New Zealand decided later not to lodge a complaint about Dallaglio's attack.

As England's coach, Clive Woodward, talked in the rooms of losing the most intense test of his career there was a terrific crash from above. "That is Jonah coming out of the shower," said Woodward, joking through his pain.

Such a triumph meant New Zealand's 43-31 loss to France in the semi-final was even more of a disaster. It was simply the greatest upset in the history of the World Cup, and in All Blacks history. Lovers of superlatives described it as the most colossal upset in the history of sport. The Scottish soccer seer, Tom Shankly, summed up such strong feelings back in 1981, when he said, "Some people think football is a matter of life and death...I can assure them it is much more serious than that." Vince Lombardi, the renowned American gridiron coach, put it this way: "Winning isn't everything, but wanting to win is." The truth perhaps is, the French really wanted to win. The All Blacks lost the white-hot passion that wins ultimate prizes.

The build-up to this awesome game had been unusual and fuelled later criticism. The All Blacks headed to the south of France for three days of team bonding. "Other halves", as partners, wives and girl friends are known, stayed behind, except for Jonah's girlfriend, Teina Stace. While the boys played golf she and Jonah strolled hand-in-hand. A former All Black later said from the safety of anonymity that this team "couldn't make up their mind whether they were playing footy or on a piss trip." Chris Laidlaw had warned earlier in the year that Jonah's sense of position on the field had always been a weakness. Opponents exploited this, he cautioned, and the French had almost made an art form of it.

Not that any of this appeared to affect his

on-field performance. Split by disagreements over the team selection, described as lacking imagination, impetus or even decent management, it was France who had everything to prove at Twickenham. After being roused by their soul-shaking anthem, *La Marsellaise*, the French played like men divinely inspired, their forwards breaking a once impregnable defence. The ball was quickly fired out to the backs who let loose with short kicks to find a way through the All Blacks. Winger Christophe Dominici scored the first two tries, zigzagging through the defence. Standing just 1.71metres, he is a fearless tackler. "Obviously you cannot compare me with Lomu," he says. "He relies on his physical qualities, but mentally he's not that strong. In a way, that's normal. If he was aggressive and could tackle well, it would be too much."

Although French players swarmed all over Jonah like fierce bull ants he scored two tries by half-time, one that would have probably been impossible for any other player. The ball sped from Jeff Wilson to Jonah then back to Wilson, and on again for Jonah to finish. The All Blacks were up 24-10. Jonah's typical player scattering dash, described by one writer as resembling the charge of an enraged rhinoceros, left six would-be tacklers either grounded or still hanging off him. His second try, just after the break, came when French fullback Xavier Garbajosa became one of many who chose the discretion of a sidestep over a tackle. Yet three French tries and 33 points, including two dropped goals, broke the All Blacks in twenty-six brilliant minutes.

France, who had been written off because of their suspensions, dissension, injuries and lack of form, received a standing ovation from the 70,000 Twickenham crowd. To put this match into perspective France had been bottom in the European Five Nations championship the previous season and had been thrashed 54-7 by New Zealand in Wellington the previous June. Again commentators found that Jonah had been under-used. But he was there, with just five other All Blacks, to congratulate the French as they disappeared in euphoria down the players' tunnel.

In Paris tooting cars jammed the Champs-Elysee and the headlines read: "France beats Lomu." *Le Monde*, a newspaper so staid that it once declined to carry photographs on its front page, was exultant about what it says was "one of the most beautiful matches in history." Prime Minister Jacques Chirac was quickly on the phone to captain Raphael Ibinez. France had already won the World Cup in soccer under their captain, Didier Deschamps, who was going wild in the stands at Twickenham. This was greater even than his stunning victory. "We knew we could do it, we were playing at home," he exulted. "But they achieved the impossible."

Jonah, 'the extra terrestrial one' the French called him, had been up against Phillippe Bernat-Salles, who gave away five years, 15 centimetres and 38 kilograms to Jonah. When Tana Umaga in utterly uncharacteristic fashion dropped a vital All Blacks ball, Magne and Bernat-Salles booted it 70 metres down the field, scooting on to beat winger Jeff Wilson to the ball and score. The match had been presented to the sporting world as a heavyweight contest along the lines of the Tyson and Hollyfield bout. Bernat-Salles, on the other hand, thought back to 1995 when he played for the French Barbarians in Toulon and twice got past Jonah.

After it was all over this time little Bernat-Salles emerged from the changing-room. He had encountered a naked Jonah. "Me," he said, "I wore a t-shirt because frankly I knew the difference." Tucked under the Frenchman's arm were some sweet souvenirs of this astonishing victory: Jonah's jumper shorts and socks. Jonah had Phillippe's jersey. France lost to Australia in the final and Jonah was generous in his praise of the conquering Wallabies.

By the time South Africa beat New Zealand 20-18 in the play-off for third place the joke going round was that All Black was entirely appropriate for a nation deep in mourning. As Jonah once said: "What we hate most is coming second best to ourselves." When this was put to Michael Jordan, the greatest player in basketball history, he replied: "I don't mind being second best to myself. Because then I'd be number one *and* two."

The loss to France did serve as a catalyst for Jonah staying in New Zealand when he could have earned more money elsewhere. "It had a lot of influence on my decision, because financially it was around the other way," he told reporters. "What tipped the scales was what was going to make Jonah Lomu happy - and that is playing for New Zealand. It is unfinished business for us now. A lot of the players who played at the World Cup know it is unfinished business. I want to give something back to New Zealand rugby and I really want to play for the All Blacks again. Why New Zealand?

You could say it is the silver fern: once you've had a taste of it you want more. I've had four years of it, though some of it is on and off, I still want to taste it and that is what tipped the scales. That is what it is about." His contract has an option of two extra years, which would take him up to the World Cup in 2003. Among other offers, British Super League Club Wakefield Trinity had dangled a two-year $3 million contract in front of him.

There was, however, more than love of the silver fern that kept him home. He moved from the Waikato Chiefs to sign a two-year contract with Wellington Hurricanes (his third Super 12 team in as many years) in the hometown of his girlfriend Teina Stace. This move linked him with two outstanding All Blacks, Christian Cullen and Tana Umaga, as well as the tutelage of coach Graham Mourie, considered among the finest international captains since the Second World War, and another pre-eminent All Black of the seventies, Bryan Williams.

Williams found that Jonah is slow over distance, but not surprisingly, is stronger than a front row prop. Jonah clocked a modest 17 minutes 3.5 seconds over three kilometres, even though he put in 5.83 seconds for 50 metres in a fitness test with the Hurricanes. Jonah's slowness over distance did not worry Williams, however. "His speed was awesome, and so was his strength – he was stronger than the props." Jonah had been weary after spending two nights in an Auckland hospital where his father Semisi had been ill.

5

A Different Kidney

THE NEWS OF Jonah's illness in 1997 was so devastating because it was so unexpected. Everything had been going nicely for him during 1996. He was playing Super 12 with the Auckland Blues, then almost an All Blacks side. In one match eight players dangled from the man of stone as he kept going forward. The Blues won an astonishing final against Natal, leading Laurie Mains to join the chorus of those who have said that Jonah, with his pace and power, could perform unrivalled feats on the rugby field. Later, though, Jonah began to notice that cuts were not healing.

A minor blood disorder had been diagnosed before the tour of France and Italy in 1996. When fresh abnormalities emerged, the All Blacks' doctor, John Mayhew, had Jonah consult Ian Simpson, a kidney specialist. Simpson broke the news to Kingsley Jones that Jonah had to undergo a six months course of chemotherapy.

Suddenly the most famous rugby player in the world was reduced from hero to victim, and a severely damaged victim at that. On Friday 24 January 1997 radio and television shows in New Zealand were interrupted with the news that he had been suffering from nephrotic syndrome for at least eighteen months. Jonah put on a positive face at a press conference. "I've got the best doctors on the case and I never lie down and let anything trample over me," he said. "This is just a hiccup." The condition arises from malfunctioning kidneys. This leads to a swelling of the body, a high cholesterol level and a higher danger of infection. Mike Turner, a British sports medicine specialist, said that for a young athlete it was like being shot between the eyes. That opinion served to wipe away the positive public relations work constructed around Jonah's illness.

His treatment involved a controlled use of steroids and a course of drugs similar to those used in chemotherapy treatment for people with cancer. John Mayhew, commented, "For the last eighteen months he has been sort of dragging a cart around, metaphorically. He's managed to train and play, (but) I'm not sure how." Graciousness was shown by Mike Catt, an England player trampled over by Jonah during the World Cup the previous year. To Catt this illness was disastrous both for Jonah and for rugby, simply because Jonah had done so much for the modern game "He's one of rugby's good guys, as well as being a phenomenal player."

Jonah may be one in a million as a footballer, but his illness affects one person in a hundred. To combat his condition, he had to down 14 different pills daily without choking on them. As a result of his treatment and the disease he blew out to 148kg and could scarcely bend to tie his shoelaces. For two months Jonah prayed and took his pills as his condition improved. The first time he tried running after all of this he pulled up eleven times.

Relaxed and slimmer, he did a spell as a commentator for British television at the Rugby World Cup Sevens in Hong Kong in March 1997. By then his weight was down from 122kg to what he calls his fighting weight, 115kgs, and he was talking of being as fast as ever over forty metres. He was no longer eating two chickens a day and feeling hunger pangs half an hour afterwards, which his doctor had said was normal for his condition. By now he was beginning to be overwhelmed by his frustration at being away from the game and took some of it out on a heavyweight punching bag, ripping it from its hinges.

When not venting his anger he was in a more cosmetic mood, becoming a model of a modern sporting idol. His year away from the game was also spent honing his presentation skills. Such an understated modesty enhances and spreads his popularity. Public speaking, handling the media and coping with the public at large, all of these skills had to be taught and learned as thoroughly as tackling and passing the ball. As a teenager he was so shy that he hung his head during even the briefest of interviews. Now in front of a mass media inquisition he switches, as one writer noted, from Terminator to Bambi. The result is high praise from his sponsors for Jonah's relationship with the public, and especially with youngsters. In three days in Australia he completed five speaking engagements, traveling from Brisbane to Sydney and on to three events in Melbourne. Over eighteen months he visited ten children to fulfill their dying wish. There was no publicity.

He had hoped to be playing in the National Provincial Championships by the end of July, but by now he had not played internationally since appearing for the New Zealand Barbarians against

England at Twickenham in November 1996. Richard Thompson, who marked Jonah for the North of England against the Barbarians, saw it as a challenge that he had hoped to rise to. Jonah kept switching wings and then coming through the middle. "But unfortunately it was myself who ended up a couple of times in the second row of the stands. He just swung me around and threw me away." Yet a year later, having played only two half matches and two full games since his comeback, he had fought back to be in England for the All Blacks' nine-match tour of Britain and Ireland.

By October 1997 he was able to have a run in the reserves for Counties-Manawatu. Next day he came on in the second half to help lift Counties to a one point win in the National Provincial Championships semi-finals. Yet the chances of his making the All Blacks appeared to be fading.

The word first filtered from a fund-raising dinner for the Sir Richard Hadlee Sports Trust in Christchurch in October 1997 that Jonah would tour Britain with the All Blacks the following month. And, sure enough, there he was in November before a capacity 8000 crowd at Sardis Road, Pontypridd, lining up against Wales A. In his first match for New Zealand for 15 months Jonah produced enough bone-crushing power to create familiar disarray. He was rewarded with a sixty-sixth minute try as a second-string New Zealand cleaned up 55-8. Oddly, he has yet to score against the Welsh national side, a distinction it shares with South Africa. He was try-less in the next three tests against England (25-8), Wales (42-7) and England again (26-26).

Scoring trys for the All Blacks was another matter. Australia took home the Bledisloe Cup, winning three straight matches. When defeats by South Africa were added, the New Zealanders had lost five tests in a row, their worst run since six straight losses to those nations in 1949. Jonah played in six tests in 1997, as well as one as a substitute. His try against England at Carisbrook in Dunedin in the 64-22 win had coach John Hart overcome with excitement, but Jonah showed hesitancy in the rematch, won 40-10, was replaced and used as a substitute in the 24-16 loss to Australia in Melbourne. Again, critics complained that he was too often under-used. He scored one try in New Zealand's four-point loss to the Wallabies in Christchurch.

For Jonah the lead-up to the 1999 World Cup saw him spend more time on the bench than many a magistrate. He was a substitute in the 71-13 walloping of Samoa at Albany, scoring once, in the 28-0 win over South Africa at Dunedin, the 34-15 victory over Australia at Auckland and the 34-18 defeat of South Africa at Pretoria. He also came off the bench when Australia toppled the All Blacks 28-7 in Sydney. His arrival at the Hurricanes resulted in some spectacular tries, including a kick and chase for a try against the Sharks during the 2000 season that mirrored rugby perfection.

To the gall of New Zealanders the end of 2001 saw Australia as No. 1 in a world ranking system. Since the Wallabies hold the World Cup, the Tri-nations crown and the Bledisloe Cup, this was undoubtedly fair. But the 88 ranking points separating Australia and South Africa in fourth slot showed the narrow margin between the leading international sides. Experts say that 100 points between teams in the rankings equated to about 10 points on the field.

For players such as Jonah, the grail-like goal is to regain the top spot, but what is also exciting is that there are thirty or so other nations outside the ratings that, with proper help and encouragement, could make the World Cup a truly global competition. These include Eastern

European countries, South American sides, and teams from China, the Caribbean and the Pacific. Throw in Georgia (eighteenth), Canada (once eighth), the United States, Samoa, Fiji, and Romania, and prospects are just about endless.

The passion for the game is universal. Spike Milligan, the late, great comedian, was so keen to see the All Blacks play in Ireland that he went across without a ticket. "I knew there were bound to be touts outside the ground," he wrote. "So I went around saying, `Anybody got a ticket? Anybody got a ticket? This woman came over to me and said: `Yes, I've got a ticket." I said: Well, how much?' And she said: `Two hundred pounds.' I said: `Two hundred pounds! For that amount of money I could get the most beautiful woman in Dublin.' To which she replied: `Ah, yes, but she certainly would not give you forty minutes each way with a wonderful brass band playing in the middle'."

In May 2001 Jonah scored four tries in ten minutes against Southland. Later that month he turned out for the Barbarians against Scotland at Murrayfield. Before leaving the field at the fifty-eighth minute he had scored four tries and helped make three others. Others keenly appreciate his play in the Barbarians with insight, such as the

French international Thomas Castaignede. Early in 2002 he was contemplating his seemingly never-ending recuperation from a snapped Achilles tendon rupture suffered against Australia in November 2000. Castaignede, who plays with the English Saracens club, was anticipating his first game in 18 months. After that he was hoping for a match with the Barbarians. 'As long as they put Jonah Lomu alongside me,' he wrote in the London *Guardian*, 'I'll be fine; all I have to do is pass the ball to him and no one will notice that I'm not 100 per cent.' Castaignede showed what sometimes must be endured when he wrote that one of his skins grafts was rejected, so he had a hole in his calf through which his doctors pulled out his Achilles tendon with a pair of tweezers so that it could regenerate naturally. Castaignede did get his wish a few months later when both Jonah and Christian Cullen were named in a Barbarians squad to play England, Wales and Scotland in the middle of 2002.

Jonah returned home for five Super 12 matches in 2001, including a losing final against Canterbury Crusaders. Yet this proved to be the platform for a return to the All Blacks to again take on Australia. Those who were among the 109,874 crowd at Olympic Stadium, Sydney, in July 2001,

Jonah Lomu

marvel at this game. Three converted tries within six minutes had the All Blacks up 21-0 against the world champions. After one minute and 29 seconds Tana Umaga on the wing intercepted Chris Latham's pass to score from 45 metres out. From the restart Jonah charged through, then unloaded for Pita Alatini to score. At five minutes and three seconds, centre Alama Ieremia burst weak tackling for a try by the posts. Then Australia counter-attacked to be level at half time.

Twice in the second half Australia led. With a few minutes to go Australia was ahead 35-34, then New Zealand secured possession on their half. It was down to three minutes when captain Taine Randell drew two tacklers then released to Jonah on the 22-metre line hard against the left touchline. The Wallabies halfback Stephen Larkham had Lomu lined up. Jonah broke free of Latham's flailing arms, turned on the turbos, then he was over and so was the match.

Jonah gave New Zealand a perfect start against Australia with a second-minute try in August 2001 at Carisbrook, Dunedin. This ground has earned the second-hand epithet of House of Pain, the original tag being used in the 1950s for Boston Gardens then the home of the formidable Boston Celtics basketball team, but now no more.

Australia engineered a remarkable recovery to win at Carisbrook, by a single point and the first time in 96 years on this ground. Their reward was to take home the Bledisloe Cup.

The following month Jonah beat two Australian tacklers, then flicked the ball inside to Alatini who had a clear run. In spite of these efforts, the Wallabies triumphed once more. A try by Toutai Kefu in the final minutes again gave Australia a win. In September a team called Leeds Rhinos came a-knocking with an interesting offer for Jonah to play rugby league for its side and union for Leeds Tykes. By now the offers were piling up, but the black jersey was still his most prized possession.

Before he ran out against Ireland in November 2001 some commentators suggested that no longer did Jonah resemble the awesome threat of legend. In the rooms he had been so nervous that he vomited. Thus it was all the more unbelievable when an Irish player booted the ball straight into Jonah's hands to set up an unstoppable try. Two deadly Jonah assists rendered any debate on his legendary status irrelevant. Working as a fearsome combination with Josh Kronfeld, Jonah either scored or created a try every time he touched the ball. He still meant business – on and off the field.

6

Keeping up with Kingsley

IN 1996 PHIL KINGSLEY JONES formed No. 11 Management, handling Jonah's sponsorship deals, appearances and other business. Jonah's parents work for the firm, as does Kingsley Jones's daughter. It was set up on a handshake basis between Jonah and his manager, as Jonah says, "I do what I have to do on the field and he does everything else off the field."

Kingsley Jones has had his ups and downs. He has been both a comedian with Butlin's holiday camps in Britain and a pie salesman in Auckland. He is gifted with native shrewdness and is clearly loyal. "Where he goes, I go," he says of Jonah. When Jonah asked him to manage him he also asked him to name his price. "I said I only wanted one thing, his next All Blacks jersey," was the Welshman's reply.

Kingsley Jones showed his manager's

determination to keep what is Jonah within his domain, declining to answer simple questions or cooperate on this book and he was unwilling to allow his charge to be interviewed, saying instead that a book on Jonah would be coming from Britain after the 2003 World Cup. "I'm a stubborn Welshman and I don't dance to anybody's tune," he said when Jonah's contract was being negotiated in 2001. "I know what's he's worth. His image is worth a fortune."

Image, of course, is a public relations term, but it clearly fascinates Kingsley Jones. He said of Jonah and the All Blacks, worrying not a whit about redundancy: "What we are trying to get together is the two strongest images in world rugby and combine them. It sounds simple, but it's more difficult than that."

Kingsley Jones's countryman, the Australian classicist and critic, Dennis Pryor, once described sport as the DNA of television. Networks spend millions trying to uncover the genetic map of viewers in order to modify their viewing genes. Jonah proved to be an ideal catalyst for a genetic code change. Few athletes achieve the awards heaped on him in 1995. Voted Player of the Tournament at the World Cup, he was the first All Black in 90 years to score four tries in a test match against England. While one British newspaper hailed him as Overseas Sportsman of the Year, the BBC named him its Television Sportsman of the Year. He was the British and European Rugby Writers' Player of the Year, New Zealand Sports Personality of the Year and picked in rugby writers' Greatest Ever World Rugby Team for the year.

With fame came a scrum of sponsors eager to cash in on his heroism. In the early days McDonald's, Reebok, Mazda and PowerAde boosted his income. Mazda and PowerAde pulled out before the 1995 triumph. Now it is adidas, with $150 million for the All Blacks and $12 million over two years for Jonah, as well, a car stereo company called Fusion, Sony Playstation, a record company and Enza, a New Zealand fruit and cool store company pushing apples, that boost his income by an estimated $4 million a year. The NZRFU pays him $360,000 to play and for appearances. Later an ice-cream company, in the febrile abuse of English, named him as an ambassador for "a new, indulgent range for adults and special dessert." A positive aspect of Jonah touting ice cream was that an unstated percentage was pledged by both sides of this deal to be donated to Jonah's favourite charity, Kidney Kids of New Zealand.

His deal with adidas includes a top-to-toe playing and training outfit deal, except when he plays Super 12, where his Wellington Hurricanes must wear the rig of sponsors Canterbury. Globally, adidas lined him up with Anna Kournikova, Martina Hingis and golfing prodigy Sergio Garcia in a self-improvement campaign. For adidas, whose target audience is aged between 12 and 20, the result put the rugby man at No.1 in terms of projecting the aim of the campaign and the running shoe to which he was aligned. Craig Lawson, adidas' New Zealand managing director, held that it was vital for Jonah to be an All Black, but saw it as more than just about the game. "It's more about having an icon in the sport, and it doesn't matter where he goes, he's like a Pied Piper with kids." Jonah will tirelessly sign autographs. Eric Rush recalls him saying that it might be Jonah's two hundredth autograph for the day that was being signed, but for the youngster it may be the first.

Anyway, Jonah considers these youngsters his peers. "Basically," he remarked," I'm a big kid. I haven't grown up." What one interviewer regarded as an almost childlike affability helps make him such an effective hospital visitor. "Some people like to use this sort of thing as a publicity stunt," he says. "I like to be a genuine guy and be a friend to people in hospital. It's sad sometimes. I get mixed emotions, but putting a smile on their face, that's more than winning the lottery, that's more than playing a test match."

Adidas contributed to the stream of Jonah the whale jokes by starring him in a commercial with a large fish. In it, Jonah arrives at the scene of a car crash where a fish has been jettisoned from the car to the road. He grabs the dying fish. We see him running over the bonnet of a car, fish under his muscled arm, down an alley, through a car wash, shouldering a van aside and getting the fish to the sea.

Wearing adidas, concludes a skinny ancient, makes you more caring about fish, other creatures, and people. There is a video of the making of this advertisement, and a television news clip of Jonah answering some bone-headed questions. He does say that a rugby ball is easier to handle than a fish, especially if the fish has been around for a few days. He doesn't ask if the fish was tired.

When it comes to making money from advertising Jonah's newest near-rival in rugby is utility back Jason Robinson, joint holder of the record for scoring tries in six successive rugby league tests for Britain. Robinson switched codes and has played three times for the British Lions and appeared for England. Jonah's six-figure boot contracts in Britain make him and Robinson the only rugby players to match the footwear sponsorship fees paid to soccer players. There are further similarities: like Jonah, Robinson is known for being child friendly and averse to promoting drink or tobacco.

Jonah was further celebrated when, in 1998, he was a guest at what was called the State of the World Forum in San Francisco, where global leaders, such as Mikhail Gorbachev and Margaret Thatcher, were gathered. Jonah's role was to present an All Blacks jersey to film star Robin Williams. The big footballer hoisted up the short funny man, who described Jonah as not only articulate and committed, but also full of energy and very funny.

Jonah's global reputation grew with the publication in 1999 of *Blood and Thunder*, an unofficial biography, by English reporter Phil Shirley. Although it confuses the state of Queensland in Australia with the resort town of

Queenstown in New Zealand and is tricked out with breathless rather than deathless London Sunday paper prose about tracing Jonah's childhood gang warfare acquaintances, it is a generally sympathetic account. The book's tale of Jonah's muscular Christianity appealed especially to the War Cry, the newspaper of the Salvation Army in Britain, which reviewed it under the heading, *A man of faith and muscle*. "Ever since the five years of his childhood spent in Tonga he has learned to appreciate the simple beauty of God's creation," the critique noted. "He loves to talk with his Lord."

But on the field the inconsistent use of his formidable talents and his wasted time on the bench was taking a toll. There was a wider world lusting for his services. Even in a nation as obsessed with a single sport, as New Zealand, the news that Jonah was on the market was devastating. A Sunday newspaper splashed the story on its front page on 1 August 1999. The London club Saracens had considered a $2million a season fee.

By November London Irish and Gloucester entered the bidding, while Wakefield Wildcats rugby league club came up with what it said was a serious offer. London Irish talked almost $500,000 a year, plus $1 million from club sponsors. The ubiquitous Kingsley Jones played the agent's role with the panache of an impresario, telling English newspapers:" All sorts of other people have also approached us." He usefully noted that New Zealand at that stage probably needed Jonah more than ever, although clearly there was big money available in England. "Lomu," observed Bristol chief executive, Nick de Scossa, after long talks with the star and his manager," is a very marketable person and it is up to his management to secure other deals with sponsors and the monies from that would go directly to the player." Bristol had already recruited Springbok five-eighth Henry Honiball and Argentina halfback Agustin Pichot. Besides Bristol, Saracens, Gloucester, Worcester, London Irish and Leeds were lining up for Jonah's services.

The initial move to look abroad by Jonah followed a decision by All Blacks coach John Hart for Jonah to spend more time on the bench, coming into the game late as an impact player. But Jonah did not want to be a part-time All Black. "You can sense the frustration as the big guy prowls the touchline in his replacements' tracksuit," English rugby columnist Stephen Jones wrote during the World Cup in Cardiff. Then there were the

Jonah-for-rugby-league reports. Jones said: "You must be joking. If you want Jonah Lomu to go to English rugby league then you must be the sort who would enter your Ferrari for the local stock-car race."

To Jones there was a degree of jealousy surrounding Jonah and his mighty profile and great earnings. But Jonah's profile from the 1995 World Cup meant millions in gate receipts, television contracts and sponsorships. The hooks that catch on to Jonah can be bizarre. He has even been a topic for creationists, who hunt the world's publications seeking items that might promote evolutionary theories and then attempt to debunk them. So it was when the *Otago Daily Times* reported that the anatomy professor at the University of Otago, Phillip Houghton, had proposed that Jonah was proof of the theory of evolution. Houghton said that because of their large physiques, Polynesians were starting to dominate New Zealand rugby. The reason for this, he argued, was that their muscle bulk is on average bigger than that of other people because only a few of their forebears survived the long journey to New Zealand over a cold Pacific Ocean. Houghton noted that "in open boats, only the big and strong survive." The traditional view is that Polynesians came from Asia later than the already-settled Melanesians, but Houghton said they quickly evolved from the Melanesians and 'very recently'. As for the creationists, they noted that Houghton could be right about the boat-survival theory. But if so, they argued, the genes for great muscle bulk would had to have been already present in the ancestor population that undertook long voyages. This demonstrated natural selection eliminating genetic information, not creating anything new. "Hence it has nothing to do with assumed molecules-to-man evolution."

In spite of this academic and neo-academic theorizing, Jonah's place in the evolution of the sporting species is assured, so much so that on a website discussion on cloning humans a contributor wrote that he relished the prospect of having another one of himself. 'I donate a few cells, which are grown in a tissue culture medium. The nucleus, containing my genetic material is transferred to a human egg, which has had its nucleus removed. The new cell then starts dividing, and is impanted into a receptive uterus (I suppose it will have to be a human one at first) and a baby me is born.' The writer notes that this can be repeated time and again. 'Imagine a rugby team of fifteen Jonah Lomus! All that would be needed is a little money and fifteen surrogate mothers. The downside may be that no one would want to play rugby any more.'

A large whale in a tiny fishbowl can find much of this unbearable. A New Zealand television news editor explained that, when it came to news values, Jonah had rewritten all the rules. "The interest in him is so great that he doesn't even have to do much and it's taken notice of," said Richard Becht. Kingsley Jones, Jonah's manager and semi-custodian, notes that New Zealand doesn't have a bizarre sporting figure such as Denis Rodman, or that other media magnet, `Gazza' Gascoigne. "The nearest we have got to a young famous sportsman is Jonah and so whatever he does, it's like he's in a drug rehabilitation clinic or died his hair green or wearing women's dresses or got married for three days. He suffers for that." Kingsley Jones, with the true volubility of his race, told a London newspaper, "Anyway, he's not a womaniser. Jonah Lomu could be left with the whole Miss World contingent in their bathing costumes and Jonah Lomu would not be interested." Jonah did in fact help judge a Miss World contest. His interest or otherwise is not recorded.

7

Sevens Up

THE ALL BLACKS apart, Jonah, seems to largely reserve his passion for Sevens rugby. The slimmed-down, speeded up, version of the game suits him and sharpens his skills. As a dreadlocked teenager he had shown his pulverising form in the Hong Kong Sevens. Three years later he spent three and a half hours signing autographs while back in Hong Kong as a commentator and talked passionately about the freedom that Sevens gives him. "It's a game that expands the mind," he said. "It brings out your vision. Once you have got that vision you can take it through to 15s."

The rugby world applauded his return to full health when he inspired New Zealand Sevens to an inaugural gold medal at the 1998 Commonwealth Games in steamy Kuala Lumpur, Malaysia. As well as his kidney condition he had been coping with knee injuries, so it was an emotional Jonah who took the podium to receive his medal. With his help the Kiwis had simply hurled the Fijians aside. Now he wept. "This," Jonah said later," was my time to come back." The schoolboy phenomenon of Hong Kong in 1994 and 1995 and the dynamic athlete of the World Cup in South Africa had returned. While he failed to score, his chase and tackle against a massive Fijian was the confrontation of the tournament.

His mind-expanding was shown in force at the third World Cup Sevens at Mundalista Stadium in the Argentinian resort of Mar del Plata, in January 2001. Reduced to a small role in the early rounds, he turned the struggle for the Melrose Cup into a one-man show of power, stealth, hunger and bliss. Australia, who had eliminated the powerful Fiji in the semi finals, could not prevent New Zealand from adding to the Commonwealth Games title they had won three years earlier. Jonah scored after 40 seconds, running, in the words of Wallaby turned coach Glen Ella, over a defender as if he were a speed bump. He stormed across the line just before the break, and then completed his hat trick early in the second half when he cut inside to take a pass. "Jonah was a big part of our game plan," said

New Zealand coach Gordon Tietjens, "because he is basically unstoppable from close range." The score: 31-12.

Unless he is in town Jonah is rarely mentioned in Melbourne, home of Australian Football. One exception was when the local rugby league side, Melbourne Storm, were "Lomued" at Stadium Australia in May 2002. A distant cousin of Jonah, Andrew Lomu, who had signed with the Sydney Roosters as a fourteen-year-old, set up a try just before half-time and scored himself later. Andrew, a Tongan World Cup player, showed some devastating form in the 34-6 crushing of the Storm. Jonah himself was noted when he scored three tries to devastate Australia in the third World Cup Sevens final 34-12 win that gave New Zealand its first World Cup Sevens win in Argentina in January 2001. He continued his ferocious, almost frightening domination in New Zealand's 31-7 win over the hosts, who had surprisingly downed South Africa 14-12 in a brutal clash.

Before the final Eric Rush, the Kiwis' outstanding captain who had taken Jonah on his first Sevens expedition a decade before, was flown home for surgery after breaking his leg in the final pool game against England. Rush recalled the earlier trip to Singapore with the 14-year-old who was so big, so quick, so keen and ten years younger than the rest of the team. "In the first game we said, `We'll help you with the first kickoff, but after that you're on your own'. He scored the first try, kicked the goal and we beat this team 28-0." This time an emotional Jonah dedicated his three tries in the final to Rush. And they were typically exquisite. Two of them came in the first-half, including one of 70 metres. But how to explain him to the soccer-mad Argentinians? Local television commentators tried by calling him the Maradona of rugby, a compliment in the area of skill if not in scandal. When this was put to Jonah he gave it some thought before simply saying, "I am Jonah and he is Maradona."

At the end of May Jonah was again rampaging at Twickenham, this time for the Barbarians. The Baabaas' tours were once notable as an occasion for carousing. The clinical professionalism of rugby changed all that, and Jonah showed it as he swept through from a quick lineout, putting his side 16 points clear. In the first half hour the young England side hardly knew what hit them as Jonah and his teammates scored virtually at will, with Jonah bearing three English doll-like tacklers as he swept up the left.

The Scots, always keen to poke fun at their southern rivals, circulated a yarn about an All Blacks game against England where the score was 50-0 at half time, Jonah having scored eight tries. The rest of the team decided to head for the pub instead of playing in the second half and told Jonah that he was on his own. "No problems," Jonah told the captain. "I'll come down after the game and report back." After the match Jonah found the rest of the team at the pub.

"What was the final score, Jonah?" asked one player. "It ended up 95 points to three."

"What!!!!" exclaimed the captain. "How did you let them get three points?" Jonah replied,

"I got sent to the bin for ten minutes."

Injuries to two New Zealand Sevens players forced Jonah back to Twickenham that month. His team did the necessary again. Jonah scored once in the semi-final and in the final of the London leg of the World Sevens Series, he was replaced halfway through the second half, but not before leaving his indelible boot-print on the game. For once he was on the receiving end of a shoulder charge by Fiji's Eperama Navale. From the kick off it had needed three Fijians to bring him down. Minutes later he was unstoppable as he sped in for a try, disposing of Rupeni Qauqau on the way.

Quaqua, as sportswriters love to say, spent some time in the hands of the trainers.

The following month Jonah's manager Kingsley Jones was all over the papers crying foul after his charge was dropped from an initial squad of 22 for a test against Samoa. A sense of horror swept the country, wrote Chris Laidlaw, who added that where successive New Zealand coaches set out to fill the gaps in Jonah's attendance record, coach Wayne Smith had become openly aggressive by telling Jonah that until he eliminated his tendency to lose concentration his place was permanently at risk.

Other issues in Jonah's relegation included the Sevens tournaments that took him all over the world, promoting his interests with those of the game, according to Laidlaw. This caused some lack of coherence in the All Blacks' preparations. As well, Jonah's positional sense had always been suspect and his opponents exploited it. "The hard truth of the matter is that with the ball behind him, Jonah is more often a liability than an asset."

So instead of the match with Samoa where was Jonah to play? For Wainuiomata, a 600-member club (Motto: Striving for the Top) against Tawa in the Second Division of Wellington's premier club competition. A "gobsmacked" Kingsley Jones protested: "He doesn't need a rest: he wants to play. He's jumping out of his skin to play. Doesn't the game count, or is he not playing well enough? I don't know the answers to those questions."

There were other troubling questions, too. Did the All Blacks need a new captain? Was Jonah out in order to allow Doug Howlett and Jeff Wilson to show their stuff, or was he being punished for touring with the Barbarians and the National Sevens team? Jonah's contract stipulates that he can play Sevens or festival games when they do not conflict with his appearances in Super 12 or for the All Blacks. Whatever the case, Wynne Gray, chief rugby writer for the *New Zealand Herald*, noted: "Parents have been struggling to explain to their children that Lomu is not in the All Blacks during the very week selectors and the New Zealand Rugby Union start a fresh campaign for players to have pride in the black jersey." He went on to say that as old-timers reminisce of great players and moments in All Blacks history, with the selection of the 1000th All Black, there were those who wondered whether the lustre of All Blacks test status had just been tarnished.

Jonah himself remembered how he felt when dropped by the All Blacks in 1994, but he turned out in the club game, and unlike his appearance for the side the previous year, did not score a try. He then went home to watch the All Blacks stitch up Samoa 50-6. The following week he was recalled to the national side for a 67-19 walloping of Argentina at Christchurch, going on to play in eight more international matches that year.

He scored in a sweet 37-12 win over the old enemy, France, at Wellington, in 2001. Strangely enough, six years earlier he also scored once in Paris, where the result was exactly the same in the game that was the last for Laurie Mains as All Blacks coach. The previous year he had to return home after fracturing a cheekbone in the All Blacks First Test win over France in Paris, 39-26. Six matches later Jonah was caught in an archetypal action photo. One Scottish player has his lower left leg. A second is grabbing him from behind, while a third heads at him. Jonah is getting his pass away. Those who were at Murrayfield are unlikely to forget the terrible beauty of Jonah's game. At one stage New Zealand were inside their 22. Scottish halfback Gregor Townsend lost possession. Seizing the ball, flanker Richie McCaw whipped it to Jonah

who blasted up to the touch line, then chipped
ahead, resulting in Scottish left wing Chris Paterson
killing the ball and giving the phenomenal Andrew
Mehrtens one of his six penalty goals. With the
score at 18-6 Jonah exploded through the weary
Scots tacklers. Mehrtens released Tana Umaga for a
lovely try. Late in the game the All Backs were
again in their territory when Umaga torpedoed a
diving pass to Jonah who belted in to kiss Scotland
goodnight at 37-6, and end an unbeaten five-game
tour. By now coaches were giving him more
options. Instead of just running over the opposition
he was exploiting angles and a swerve.

Two years earlier a Scottish wing, Cammie
Murray, had jinked and twisted past Jonah as
Scotland exited the World Cup. This time Jonah ran
in four of his team's 12 tries on this same ground
when he took part in the 74-31 demolition of
Scotland by the Barbarians. It was a perfect evening
at Murrayfield as 30,000 fans honoured the
memory of their late Scottish rugby hero, Gordon
Brown. They also paid tribute to Jonah, giving him
a standing ovation when he came off after sixty
minutes. Three tries in the first ten minutes set the
scene. Soon after half time the crowd broke into
ironic applause when Murray balked at the sight of

Jonah and tried to chip over him. A maker of tries as well as a taker, Jonah set up several breaks, leading Baabaas coach Bob Dwyer to observe: "We didn't do very much, but Jonah did a lot and it doesn't surprise me how easily Jonah opened up defences."

Also noteworthy in this game was that three former New Zealanders, John Leslie, Gordon Simpson and Brendan "Chainsaw" Laney, lined up for Scotland. A former Otago fullback Laney had become a proud Scot just 11 days before the game by virtue of a grandmother who had been born in Glasgow. This would seem to make Jonah a starter for Tonga if a freakish event should toss him in that direction

The end of 2001 saw the All Blacks scrape home against Argentina. With 56,000 fans, including Diego Maradona, in Buenos Aires hysterically rending the air as the Pumas led within minutes. New Zealand had to do that something special. Jonah, who specialises in the special, scored early to give his team an 8-7 lead. The Pumas were up 10-8 at half-time however, and, after sixty-six minutes, they were leading by three points and looked like getting their first win against the men in black in 15 years. A Scott

Robertson injury-time try, converted by Mehrtens, buried the hopes and bruised the hearts of the Pumas 24-20.

8

Jonah's Game

LIKE THE BROKENHEARTED Pumas, Jonah has a simple game plan. On his video and DVD, *Jonah*, launched in 2001 and soon outselling titles from the likes of telly chef Jamie Oliver, he examines the intricate task of getting past an opponent. He studies their weaknesses and considers how much of what he calls his physical presence he will need. "I have to process that really quickly through my mind and use my strength to beat them." That, of course, is a modest summary of his armoury that includes fending off with a big hand, changing stride, swerving and running at angles. "I try to get them off balance," he says, chuckling at the thought of players who try to save face (and body) by just diving at his bootlaces. "Some of them have a go up high," he continues. "Sometimes you have no option but to go over the top of them."

Bruce Robertson, an outstanding All Blacks centre, ranks Jonah with John Kirwan when in possession, but is another who wonders whether Jonah has been used at his best. Ignoring Jonah, one All Black reckoned, would be like Manchester Untied not passing to David Beckham or the LA Lakers shunning Shaquille O'Neal.

Graham Henry, who coached the Auckland Blues to two Super 12 championships, and went on to a less successful coaching stint at Wales with a multi-million dollar contract, summed it up this way: "He's the only player who can score tries that no other player can score, whether it's at the end of the line or coming in outside second five."

Henry was known for his imaginative coaching. In the 1996 Super 12 final, Auckland Blues playing Natal, he put Jonah in the lineout. "There are players who can plant the seed of doubt in opposing teams," Henry says. "If you have Jonah on the wing in form, then you need a hell of a good winger to stop him and a centre who has to do the extra cover, and a fullback who's got to try to get up." Three players have to work out what do if Jonah gets around his man, which he does with numbing regularity. "He can do two or three things in a game that will turn it."

From the front-row of the English scrum came a blunt opinion. "I sense some of the lads didn't like the idea of having to tackle him," said Brian Moore, the acerbic Englishman. "You need confidence in sport. He knocks that rather." Kevin Campion, lock for the successful Brisbane Broncos rugby league team and a renowned tackler, was honest as well, confessing that he would simply dive in front of Jonah and pray that he tripped.

Another former All Blacks wing, Grant Batty, famously said of Jonah," I think you need an elephant gun to stop him." He went on, "People underestimate his pace. (Wallaby) Stephen Larkham has got pace and he was unable to catch him. Once Jonah has the ball in his hand and he's moving at pace, there's no better player in world rugby."

Nick Farr Jones is happy that his time as Wallaby captain was before Jonah came along. "I certainly wouldn't stand in front of him. I can't profess to know how to stop him. But those who have done so successfully in the past, like the South Africans in the World Cup, have restricted his momentum early. Other than that, grab a lasso and hang on!"

Contrast this with former All Black Earle

Kirton, who said after New Zealand's 39-35 win before 110,000 fans in Sydney on 15 July 2000: "He's the greatest game breaker I've ever seen. He gives you the opportunity to score tries, and more than anyone else who has played the game. He is awesome with the ball in hand." The All Blacks won only one of four tests against Australia and that was Jonah's.

Two tests earlier Jonah and Tana Umaga powered New Zealand to a record 69-20 thrashing of Scotland in Dunedin, a point greater than the score against South Africa three years earlier. Jonah scored three of the 11 tries. Such was the dash in the latter stages of this game that Umaga picked up a Scottish kick ahead to rip the ball to Jonah on his own goal line. With lots of space and good support he roared off, then passed to Ron Cribb for a try. From the restart Jonah shook off three defenders to finish a move started by the centre combination of Alama Iermia and Pita Alatini. Each try by these players produces elation and a ritual-style meeting of fists, resembling a clenched High Five.

Two years later the Scots were still caught by this rugby lesson. Contemplating their lack of success, a writer in the Glasgow *Herald* observed that Scotland's coach, Ian McGeechan, had exploited their strengths "but without talents like Jonah Lomu, Christian Cullen and Tana Umaga at his disposal he needs confident, in-form players to make the difference."

Michael Lynagh, one of Australia's greatest players, vigorously amplified this point. Lynagh scored 911 test points, played for the Wallabies 72 times and has a World Cup winner's medal. After the Wallabies beat New Zealand in Dunedin in what was Jonah's fiftieth test, and Australia's heroic captain, John Eales, moved towards retirement, Lynagh pondered the tactics. When the time was right, when cover and support for him was thin, Australia continually put the ball behind Jonah on the left wing. "Kicks go behind because most opposition teams know that he is not an enthusiastic chaser of balls. When the kick is to the other side of the field he does not give his team-mates the option of a counter-attack because he is not fast to get into position."

But for Lynagh, and many other watchers, there was frustration in the All Blacks' methods. 'They have the greatest attacking rugby weapon known to man,' wrote Lynagh, 'yet fail to use him in a meaningful way…He only needs to get the ball with a little bit of room and he makes yards against defence. He makes very good defences look like under-12 B graders, as he charges through their ranks. Despite international players becoming stronger thanks to advances in physical conditioning, seeing Lomu in full flight is very reminiscent of watching junior rugby matches where one of the boys has had a growth spurt and just gets the ball and runs through, around and over his less mature opposition. So why don't the All Blacks make more use of his extraordinary physical abilities?'

Of course, staunch Australians such as Lynagh particularly enjoy seeing Jonah standing out on the wing waiting for most of the game for the ball to come his way. This makes life easier for the Wallabies. 'Sometimes he gets close to the rucks to pick up the ball and run at an entire forward pack, only to be brought down very shortly after he has touched the ball,' lamented Lynagh, whose zeal for the game clearly can briefly dampen his green and gold fervour. 'What a waste.'

Were Lynagh in the All Blacks he would stand a little deeper and his first call would be, 'Get it to Jonah. I wouldn't care if the opposition heard. What are they going to do anyway? I would be using him as a decoy also. This is not done at present. Bring him in between the centres. Give him the ball sometimes, then miss him out on others.' Ideally, Lynagh wanted to see Jonah in full flight. "He needs to be given more ball in situations where he can create exactly the sort of havoc we know he is capable of creating. The other side of the coin is that he can create space for others just by being present and not even touching the ball."

David Campese, scorer of 48 tries in his 101 tests for Australia and ranked as an all-time great winger, writes of how mighty Jonah was when he had the power and speed of Frank Bunce playing inside him. 'These days outside centres seem to have a priority to crash the ball up. Getting the ball wide seems to be an after-thought,' Campese complained.

These days, too, coaches indulge in mind games before crucial matches. John Connolly, coaching the Queensland Reds, described Jonah before an important match as "half a player" 'I don't think so,' Campese responded. 'The great thing is that he can do a lot with the little ball he gets.' In the Hurricanes Jonah revels in playing in tandem with Christian Cullen, Tana Umaga and Alana Ieremia. "It's like having a big rope on the field and being able to pull the opposition from one side to the other," he says.

The game has changed so much that not only must wingers be fast and able to finish all the hard work carried out by those inside them, they must also be able to do the work of a forward when the ball is grounded, as it so often is. Once it was simpler. Vic Cavanagh, one of the greatest New Zealand coaches, reduced the game to its essential. Position, possession and pace, he said, were what it was about. Cavanagh, who coached the renowned Southern Club in Dunedin before the Second World War, handed on his skills to his son who also bore his name. In turn Vic Cavanagh Jr. instructed Laurie Mains, who went on to coach the All Blacks, South Africa's Transvaal Rugby Union and later its Cats Super 12 side and then returned to his birth place to drill the Otago Highlanders. Mains had a good record of coaching 34 All Black games for 23 wins, 10 losses and a single draw, although his record against major international sides was a loss in a third of the tests.

Another tactician, Dr Kevin Roberts, firmly holds that the ball should go quickly to Jonah in the first five minutes of a game so that he is involved early. Dr Roberts, for four years a NZRFU Board member and who at one stage commuted between New York, London and Auckland as worldwide head of the Saatchi and Saatchi advertising agency, wrote forthrightly about the game. He recalls the World Cup semi-final against England where the game plan was built around Jonah from the start and, of course, England was cleaned up. 'No one is boosting Jonah, I feel, and giving him the right kind of ball early enough,' Dr Roberts wrote. 'Lomu is capable of being the best attacking player in the world.'

Yet another form of tactics engaged Jonah when he marketed a computer game in 1997. It has consistently been praised as the best on the game. On his website he offers beanies, t-shirts, a water bottle, a calendar, aftershave, a bucket hat, a wash cap, poster, his video and DVD and, naturally, CDs of his favourite music, such as Barry White, Marvin Gaye and Warren G. Touchingly, a fan named Pierre e-mailed his website from France to offer his services as a drummer for the next CD. 'I don't actually sing on my CDs,' wrote Jonah. 'It's a selection of the music that I listen to, so thanks for the offer...' Critics have noted that Jonah has surprisingly good musical taste; with the dance floor tracks able to inspire as many neat sidesteps as a decent game of rugby. They even suggested that if his rugby career faded, he could have a good future as a wedding reception DJ.

The site appears to need attention and updating. Jonah's contributions reflect a touching naivety. At one stage he wrote of "Cassidy" Clay, the boxer. Other mistakes do mar the site, with words such as apparel in need of a spell-check. This would cause little concern to Jonah's fans, however, who were cheered by his messages to them.

E-mails to him arrive from non-rugby nations such as Greece, from Taiwan and South America, as well as the European countries, where he has many fans. This promotional magnetism is jealously guarded. Kingsley Jones, who has a small stable of sports stars, is quick to talk of litigation if be believes there has been any transgression. A giant shop window drawing of Jonah was removed from a clothing shop in New Zealand because Kingsley Jones said it had been copied from a magazine that he was suing for offering a prize of an All Blacks jersey signed by Jonah.

"Lomu," he said, "is the only sportsperson in New Zealand who has a copyright on his name and image and these can't be used without my permission." Warming to his theme, he went on, "If you opened a fish and chip shop and called it McDonald's you wouldn't last four days. What if you allowed every shop to use Jonah Lomu? There are two Jonah Lomus, rugby and business. Take (it) away from him and what's left for him after rugby?"

Which brings us to the toast sculpture. Maurice Bennett is a sculptor in Wellington, New Zealand, who attracted international attention with sculptures made by joining pieces of the staple breakfast. Bennett's toast sculpture of Jonah brought fire from that Welsh dragon, Kingsley Jones, even though the work was not for profit. Bennett sees his work as humorous, adding that if it were sold the money would go to a junior rugby team.

Amusing, as they may seem to outsiders, such incidents merely gives Jonah's critics more ammunition. Letter-writers to Wellington's newspapers accused Kingsley Jones of being precious and concerned with Jonah's business ahead of his rugby, arguing that Jonah should have been fit and ready to play for the Hurricanes early in 2002. One fan even accused him of being past his prime and not deserving such attention.

By the end of 2001 Jonah was down to two pills a day, but still watching his weight. In a week he can easily add two and a half to three kilos, so he is careful not to train excessively and stay away from the weights for a time. If he worked too much on weights he would bulk up and lose speed. He does speed and cross-training daily, weights for ninety minutes every Monday and is back in the gym later in the week to build up explosive power. A couple of hours before a big game he likes mashed potatoes, bread and spaghetti, with tomato sauce.

9

Big Man, Big Noise

IT WAS NOT FOOD but frustration that was on Jonah's mind as he fought his way back into the All Blacks late in 1997 – just about using his TV set as a football, calming down only after his wife Tanya followed her mother-in-law's example and clipped him over the ears. Tanya Rutter was an 18-year-old social work student when she and Jonah fell for each other during the 1995 World Cup in her homeland of South Africa. In defiance of the conventions of his culture and to the enormous public distress of his family, they married in a 'secret' ceremony at Manukau Harbour beach in Auckland the following March. There followed a scene that invariably is played out whenever Jonah's name is mentioned.

Politicians and other national leaders have been known to shed tears on television for differing reasons, such as confessing to alcoholism, adultery or both, leaving office when rejected by the public, or when moved by some horror. Jonah weeping on a national TV show was somehow less conceivable. Years later, when he was due to appear in the British version of *This Is Your Life*, New Zealand television replayed its file footage yet again of a weeping Jonah, his head dripping with pearl-like dreadlocks. He had been asked why he had not invited his parents to his wedding and replied: "I was scared they wouldn't let me do it." This squirm-inducing interview came before he had to confront his deeply hurt parents at their South Auckland home.

And so it came about that to make amends a second wedding was organised, this time in South Africa. The gossips were busily sharpening their daggers, regurgitating the romances of Jonah, such as the three years that Elaine Makiha was his childhood sweetheart and then an Auckland shop assistant, Leanne Russell, wore his engagement ring for a time. Then he moved on to Tanya.

Two and a half years later in 1998 Jonah left Tanya, now almost 22, for another shop assistant, Teina Stace, a 20-year-old from Wellington. Jonah followed a well-worn if somewhat rutted path by telling all to a women's magazine. The magazines breathlessly reported how Tanya had dialed into Jonah's voicemail and heard messages from Teina. Tanya moved out of the million-dollar Auckland home she had shared with Jonah and summed up their relationship by saying, "The next man would [have to] be a much better communicator." Nor would he be a sportsman.

The divorce was expensive, although in 2000 Jonah was the only present-day player to make his country's top 10 rugby rich list, with $3 million left after the split. By contrast, a former All Black turned celebrity, Andy Haden, clocked in at $4million. Grant Fox, the legendary All Black and now a television commentator, says that playing for his country opened a lot of doors, although capitalising on this was not always easy. "Once you're inside," he added, "you have to be pretty sharp to carry on."

Teina injected more off field drama into the life of Jonah while he was in Wales for a Barbarians game against South Africa in December 2000. Although she only had a learner driver's licence she was alone when she crashed his powerful Ford Falcon XR6 ten metres down an embankment near their Wellington home, breaking her right arm and getting bruised. Teina, by now 22, pleaded guilty to a charge of careless use of a motor vehicle and was sent on a defensive driving course by Justices of the Peace. After the course she was discharged without a conviction. Once together again, Jonah and Teina were able to luxuriate in a romantic week on the Tokoriki Islands, in the Mamanuca group of Western Fiji.

In 1999 New Zealand was abuzz with talk of Jonah and what the papers called his whale of a car. His British-built TVR sports car was said to be worth $300,000, although some estimate its worth at a much lower figure. Later his passion turned to drag racing. "I already drive one of the fastest street-legal cars in New Zealand, and I'm building a full stock, top-door slammer that I'm keen to race down the quarter-mile." The car's accoutrements are also intriguing and unusual. A girlfriend once talked of how he still carried in the car a cuddle bunny and bear. Said Jonah, "They're called Mr Bear and Mr Bunny." No one asked him more about them.

The world record attempt that has really rocked sports fans, however, was Jonah's push for the loudest car stereo on earth, which stood at 176 decibels. "It's basically a competition to produce the loudest possible car stereo in a form of drag racing," he explains. "Two cars line up against other and off you go. When the lights hit green, you've got thirty seconds to get the music to go as loud as you can. You wear earplugs, but even so it is highly advisable not to be even sitting in the car when the music goes on. You have to stand at least fifty metres away."

Jonah gets behind the wheel of a Nissan Patrol, number plate MACDAD, with a $100,000 sound system with nine amplifiers, capable of belting out 163 decibels. His speaker system, the Jonah 11 Fusion, reaches 165 decibels. Now, 80 decibels can cause hearing loss. A Boeing 747 taking off puts out 148 decibels. When his Nissan is not in a competition, Jonah takes out a computer chip that cuts it to one amplifier. This still sets off house burglar alarms 100 metres away. He is serious about the car audio business. To placate his neighbours, he takes his car audio system to the airport or into a large warehouse. Even his home system, however, can cause his windows to rattle and almost threatens to make the door handles fall off. The All Blacks sponsors Ford, moved Jonah up a gear in 2002 with an all-American pick-up truck. This black T-250 is powered by a 7.3 litre V8 turbo diesel engine and is said to be able to tow 4.5

tonnes, or about six hefty scrums. As for those headphones, the big bumpers he calls them, that seem to be in place almost everywhere but on the field, he admits to taking them into the showers. On the way to a game he has them pounding. "You can just hit one good song, push the right button and off you go. If I hit the right song with the right tone and the right rhythm, then bang – I'm away. When you're running you get the beat in your head and it really gets the blood pumping."

As a young player for Counties he nominated his girlfriend as his most enjoyable tackle. This was back in 1997 when he said his ideal job was sleeping and what he most enjoyed at school was to "study Sega". And what would he be doing if he had an hour with a ruck machine? Start a barbecue with it, naturally.

The fans were told that he relaxes with his favorite TV show, 'The Simpsons', and has two idols, Mohammed Ali and Elvis Presley. Ali is also the person he nominates as the man he would most like to meet. In his prime Ali was devastatingly quick. Unlike Jonah, however, he had the glib gift of hyperbole, famously saying: "I'm so fast that last night I turned off the light switch in my hotel room and was in bed before the room was dark."

To escape the pressure of his life Jonah heads out with his 9ft 8in surfboard, playing volleyball, or swooping through mangrove swamps on his jet ski. At the table his favourite dish is taro (a tuberous herb cooked by boiling and a traditional Polynesian staple), corned beef and lots of greens. He has a fondness for a rare steak, but says he tries to keep to cereal, Chinese noodles, sushi and lots of apples (his doctor has told him bananas are too rich in potassium). He sometimes nips into a McDonald's, but his knowledge of food has its limits. "The only pasta I enjoy is pizza," he memorably said. He does whip up a meal of chop suey for his parents and cook a barbecue for his rugby mates.

Tri-lingual (English, Tongan and Maori) he is famous for his passion for music, said to be more than a little inspired by Elvis-crazy aunts. One aunt in particular introduced him to music when he was just six. She used to take him to dances as her "escort" because she was not allowed to go with boys. Her mother would scrutinise her carefully as she danced with little Jonah then, as soon as the watchful eye was gone, Jonah would be told to sit down. At home he would sleep with a radio under his pillow and became a lover of the likes of Lionel

Ritchie, Barry White and Marvin Gaye, then shared one of his uncle's passions for reggae and Bob Marley, until getting into rap in the early 80s. Later Janah Jackson, Lauren Hill, TLC, LL cool J, Puff Daddy, The Strong Islanders and Naughty by Nature excited him.

Jonah makes the most of his hair. Pictured when young, he has a handsome crop. Later came a goatee. At one stage it was shaved, except for his number 11 trademark razored into the back. No. 11 has been shaved into his left eyebrow. Then came the tuft. A little patch sticks up at the front. This, too, has been controversial and one stage in 1997 it vanished to be replaced in several games by a gold-braided topknot.

Back came the tuft. Is it, as many Kiwis say, "rude"? During 2000 a bunch of senior All Blacks, led by Taine Randell actually confronted Jonah on the team bus. From a distance they called for the removal of the tuft because it was gay. Four years before All Black Glenn Osborne had a go at shaving it off while Jonah was asleep, but giggled so much he awoke the great man. The tuft will remain until Jonah decides otherwise.

10

Bigger than
the All Blacks

THE TUFT WAS bigger than ever a year before the 2002 British Commonwealth Games in Manchester, England, where a nine-storey high poster of Jonah was draped from a building in the heart of that city. As crowds watched a cherry picker hoisted Jonah, topped by a yellow hard-hat, to where he stood, about the size of one of his pictured boot studs, to spray-paint a massive autograph.

Manchester needed to sell Games tickets for its 10 days in July and Jonah, with super swimmer Ian Thorpe and heptathlete Denise Williams, were central to the lure. Another vehicle to hype Jonah was his appearance in the Sevens Rugby. Jonah even raced against Britain's Linford Christie over 60 metres to help spruik Manchester. With the likes of Olympic gold medallist Cathy Freeman, Jonah was named as one of the five stars to watch at Manchester.

As carefully covered by the organisers as the building, however, was the fact that Jonah would probably not be playing there. The NZRFU told this writer that Jonah would almost certainly be playing in the Tri-Nations instead, as the All Blacks tried to wrest supremacy back from the Wallabies. A couple of months before the Games, Jonah carried the Games torch its final New Zealand lap.

This English visit found him behind a desk signing autographs for 60 children aged from twelve to sixteen who were winners of a contest involving New Zealand apples, run by the Sainsbury department store chain. Interestingly, idols such as Tiger Woods have clauses in their contracts barring such organised autograph sessions, but Jonah smiled and chatted as he signed each with an individual message. Only when he stood to switch jumpers did onlookers comprehend his size, and glimpse the number 11 tattoo over his heart.

In New Zealand the game has always been about the team, not the individual. In all his public statements Jonah sticks to this credo, but if there is some smouldering resentment towards him, especially in the South Island where the mere mention of his name can provoke an angry exchange, it is because he is so dominant.

Just as Australian cricket's Invincibles cannot be imagined without the overwhelming presence of Don Bradman, or the great Chicago Bulls minus Michael Jordan, the All Blacks without Jonah would be diminished.

While other All Blacks have to work with their rugby union's marketing strategy, Jonah's contract stipulates that the NZRFU must get permission to use his services. The global impact of Jonah was well shown in 1999 after he re-signed with NZRFU for two more years. The Cable News Network-Sports Illustrated website polled its users on his decision. From Mobile, Alabama, Tevis VanDerGriff, wrote to applaud the decision, as a player and a fan. 'I wish others would stay for the `love of the game' instead of leaving for the "greed of the game".' Londoner Chris Horwood cheered for Jonah. 'As he said last time he was scouted, he was raised by the NZRFU, so why should he desert them and all the fans just for money.'

From Hawaii Haunga Petelo wrote unaware that Jonah was born in New Zealand to say that he was proud of his decision to remain loyal to his adopted country. Interestingly, Petelo joined the chorus in saying that if only Jonah had received more ball with ample space, the result against France in the 1999 World Cup may have been different.

Kenyan Richard Mukatha took another view, arguing that the All Blacks could produce new talent without having to rely on Jonah 'Lomu should go on with his life and let the world see the game's best player in action in the world's richest league!' Greg Sikroski in Ohio was pleased to see that, with so much money in professional sport, an athlete deciding against the lure of instant wealth. 'Mr Lomu will earn enough to keep him happy, and with his gesture, he has made himself a respected figure by sports fans throughout the world. We don't complain that athletes are paid well, but we do object to their demanding so much more than their talents merit. Mr Lomu is the best in his sport, and he has now become the most reasonable.'

Californian Daniel Sands believed Jonah would regret leaving the All Blacks without having won a World Cup. 'He plays for pride, the honour of wearing his country's jersey, something we in the U.S. have forgotten.' This did not sit well with Bill from Mesa, Arizona, who wrote: 'Screw rugby; at

6ft 5 inches and 260 lbs Jonah needs to come here to America and join the NFL. Any team would sign him and with his strength and speed he would make ten times the money he does playing rugby, even though he has never played American football. The lowest paid player in the NFl makes 300 thousand a year; Jonah could make a million a year before he ever puts on pads.' Jonah enjoys watching the American game. "I loved `The Fridge' (William Perry, the former Chicago Bears defensive tackle), the way he would run over things, I follow the Pittsburgh Steelers, the Dallas Cowboys and the San Francisco 49ers. I wouldn't mind being a running back one day."

Jonah has been asked whether he would follow former All Blacks Ian Jones and Josh Kronfeld to play professional rugby in Europe. While acknowledging that this was indeed an option, Jonah put his dilemma simply: you can't win the World Cup playing in Europe because the NZRFU would not pick overseas players. Kingsley Jones has publicly pondered whether this would survive a court challenge.

Just before Christmas in 2001 Jonah received a further honour. A world rugby side was chosen from an idiosyncratic statistical analysis of all 2000 games involving Six Nations and Tri-Nations, but excluding the Lions losing Test series against Australia. Jonah, centre Tana Umaga and fullback Leon MacDonald were the only three New Zealanders in a team that had five England players, three Frenchmen, an Irishman and a Springbok. Few fans took such a selection seriously, but the big fellow was still there.

Yet while Jonah is held up internationally as an ideal to strive for, criticism follows him and probably always will. Slow to turn, say his Kiwi judges. His work rate isn't always what it should be. His defence is poor. A New Zealand Member of Parliament, Willie Jackson, reacted angrily to the criticism. Jackson, a former broadcaster and an Alliance MP who has been regarded as a Maori activist, said that the world acknowledged Jonah as one of the best, if not the best, player in the world. "But in New Zealand people are always getting stuck into him. The continued criticism of him is astounding. It verges on racism." Long after making this statement Jackson told this writer he had no reason to change his opinion.

A lighter view is offered by the Samoan born New Zealand satirist Oscar Knightley, who wrote, 'If you were to believe all the stereotypical stuff about Pacific Islanders, you'd think they were all a bunch of laid-back-to-the-point-ofbeing-lazy-thick-shy-and-retiring-Bible-bashers, who are only good for running the ball down the wing.' A respected author and broadcaster, Phil Gifford, put it this way: 'The strikes against Jonah seem to have been driven to a large degree by the fact that so much of his life is lived in the headlines.' Jonah's loud cars and giant earphones were an affront to a culture of short back 'n' sides, gray trousers and beer.

The arguments are conducted among fans on websites such as team.sport.com, where Jonah has been called over-hyped. This brought a Kiwi response that Jonah is still arguably the best attacking player in world rugby and definitely the best winger. 'Sure he has weaknesses, but he also scores and creates tries that nobody else can,' wrote a fan. 'He is intimidating – when he scored the try to win the test match in Sydney in 2001, Stephen Larkham was thinking, How do I stop him? not, I have to stop him. He has upped his work rate, too...' Another fan was troubled by the fact that crowds in the Northern Hemisphere cheer whenever Jonah was tackled. An angry New Zealander had this to say: 'if you knew anything about rugby, you would know that the primary objective of a wing is as an offensive weapon. Kick the ball behind Jonah and he may take some time getting to it, but then I don't know of too many 6ft 4in 18st men who are as agile. Fact is, a commentator who knows and has seen a bit of rugby, Bill McLaren, in the process of choosing his best 15. Guess whom he chose as his two best left wings? Campo and Jonah. Guess what else? What do these two have in common? They score tries.'

Richard Thompson, who marked Jonah for the North of England against the Barbarians, saw it as a challenge that he had hoped to rise to. Jonah kept switching wings and then coming through the middle. "But unfortunately it was myself who ended up a couple of times in the second row of the stands. He just swung me around and threw me away."

There is no doubt that Jonah has trouble fielding balls over his head, does not kick as well as he might and is no good taking a pass while standing still. Some commentators have even suggested that he should be used in the middle to crash forward, suck in several defenders, and then pass to a free player. All he can do in reply is to play well. When he gets the ball three or four times in a game with some room between him and the defence he can usually score twice.

Looking again at some of the footage of Jonah in action against the Wallabies provides a fresh insight into his powerful defence. Here he is holding up a ball carrier just short of the try line, denying Australia a try. In the national provincial competition he is seen using his enormous strength to prevent the ball being grounded on the try line.

There will always be critics. Among New Zealand rugby journalists T.P. (Sir Terry) McLean has the status of a guru. His pronouncement on Jonah was hedged with typical caution: 'Admittedly he carries his considerable fame with a decent demeanour,' he wrote. 'But sensational? Jonah is really half a rugby player. Ten, 15, 20 metres from his own goal line attacking he is massively dangerous. But 10, 15, 20 metres from his own goal line he can cause grown men to grow pale, even terrified.' Then comes the acid: 'He has not the notion of a tackle or a well-timed dive to trap the ball. His catching, whether of a punt or a pass, can be sketchy. These deficiencies are indefensible in a great player, let alone a sensational one.'

These failings have not, of course, dimmed his scoring record and his try making. For his part,

Jonah does not believe there is any player, past or present, who is the perfect wing. Australian David Campese comes close, such were his amazing skills, but he had defensive flaws. The techniques are certainly highly polished these days, leading to an increased level of skill. "In training you have to work on all of your skills and speed training is essential, especially 40 metre to 50 metre runs" Jonah says. "As a wing during a game you're never required to run something like three kilometres non-stop." Instead, wings train like sprinters, including many power drills and exercises to help quick recovery. Like any professional sport, rugby is increasing its use of techniques that suit the game.

"Now training is more rugby specific. I keep working on my kicking. At times I have to do a full-back's job." Jonah has been developing his chip kick as an option if outnumbered. He is constantly trying to increase his options. "The more I play on the wing," he said, "the more fascinating I find it."

Early in 2002 Jonah was being kept in cotton wool by the Hurricanes. He rejoined them only at the start of February, three weeks before the start of Super 12. Clearly there were murmurings, for on his website Jonah says there had been a misunderstanding about his start for the season. Before Christmas he had talked to the All Blacks management and been assured that he was among a group of players who did not have to train until the start of February. "I really would have loved to have played in the Sevens in Wellington, but as I was not needed, I had no choice but to take a break."

By March that year, however, Jonah had to do extra sprint work with the Hurricanes to get up to speed. At most training sessions he had up to forty-five minutes additional sprint work as he headed towards his 50-match milestone in Super 12. Not until round seven did he score his first try for the Super 12 season, and that in a losing match against the Highlanders at Carisbrook. The rest of the season was disappointing with the Hurricanes failing to reach the finals and Jonah out with injury as the semi-finals approached, casting doubt over whether he would travel with Christian Cullen to play for the Barbarians in England, Scotland and Wales. The All Blacks games scheduled straight after this had greater priority. Across the Tasman there was a fierce focus on the performance of former Broncos rugby league star, Wendell Sailor, who had switched to union and was being promoted as a potential rival to Jonah in the

Wallabies. Sailor said: "I've got to make sure I do the little things well, as it's a whole different world playing someone like Jonah."

One of the diversions of various codes of football is the fantasy team. Newspapers use them as circulation builders and they can be fun. Picture, this, then: Jonah, the rugby union juggernaut, ball tucked into his catcher's mitt of a left hand is streaming towards the try line. Who can stop him? How about George Bush, leader of the free world and fullback? It isn't all that bizarre because the President is one of three occupants of the White House who played rugby at university level.

To the doubtless delight of sports loving trivial pursuit nuts, Bill Clinton and Teddy Roosevelt are the others. Both Bush's swank private school in Andover, Massachusetts, and Yale University have significant traditional links with the great game. Bush played at fullback at Yale, so he would have been in the position to try to bring down Jonah, ball and all. Would he have succeeded? Followers of the game recall how the South African fullback, Percy Montgomery, somehow went missing when Jonah headed his way and who can blame him?

Whenever Jonah is asked about aspects of

his life, his replies are disarmingly simple. His favourite sports maxim, for instance, is, "Have a dream and then follow it." He has succeeded. Even when his shorts were embarrassingly torn off when he was playing for the Auckland Blues against Natal in 1996 they were auctioned with the money going to a children's hospital. The shorts had ended in the mud, but were grabbed by Graham Thorne, a former All Black turned TV commentator. Jonah has been quoted as saying, "My heart is an open book before God. I talk to the Lord often, even before games. I ask Him to protect all the players."

By the end of his playing career Jonah wants to have done everything mentally and physically possible to help New Zealand win the World Cup that slipped from his grasp in 1999. At the end of 2001 he reflected that under the direction of new coach John Mitchell the inexperienced All Blacks had beaten Ireland, Scotland and Argentina. Yet a lot else was happening. Tana Umaga had questioned New Zealand's desire to win and even challenged the need for the season-prolonging Super 12 competition. New Zealanders look across the Tasman and see a nation that expects to win on or in sand, grass, snow, water, court, track and pitch and agonise over whether the All Blacks have lost that self-belief. Mitchell talks of looking for ten "pieces of glue" in a team, players apart. His players have to fit into that glue. He uses the jargon of management, talking of "growing" people, of co-creation and empowering the team and, where appropriate, rebuilding the team culture. So long as he gets results, it is safe to assume that this jargon will be tolerated.

If in 2003 the All Blacks fail again in the World Cup, Jonah will reassess his future. His New Zealand contract runs out that year, when he also turns 28. He excited newspapers in London at the end of 2001 by hinting that he would still consider a career in British rugby league after the World Cup. The likelihood is that he will almost certainly quit international rugby if New Zealand win. As he said, as 2001 was finishing, "That would be the scenario and hopefully it works out. I won the World Cup Sevens this year and that was a goal I reached, now I've set myself for getting the last goal, which is that World Cup in 2003. My contract with New Zealand finishes two days after the World Cup is over and we'll see where I go from there."

His All Blacks were certainly given a powerful imperative to compete fiercely for the World Cup when bickering broke out early in 2002 over the staging of the tournament. Originally it was to be held in both Australia and New Zealand. A murky dispute arose over advertising at grounds and sponsors' boxes. New Zealand fell out of favour with the International Rugby Board and in spite of an offer of help from its Government, lost the matches. Australia won all the World Cup games, leaving New Zealand impotent with rage and feeling betrayed by their cousins. Calls to boycott the Cup were succeeded by cooler demands that New Zealand concentrate on getting to the finals, then thrashing Australia, if they made it. Jonah stayed clear of such messy rugby politics. The only way forward for him was towards the try line.

This confirms the belief that Jonah, for all his enigmatic qualities, has always wanted an uncomplicated life. He has simply said that he would like to be thought of as a guy who loved to play the game, while consistently repeating that he could not be an All Black if he played outside his country. He may still follow the well-worn track of so many internationals to the northern hemisphere, where a warmer welcome surely awaits him than in many parts of his homeland. Such an outcome would leave New Zealand much the poorer, and duller.

THE JONAH LOMU RECORD

Born	12 May, 1975, Auckland, NZ
Height	1.9m (6ft. 5in.)
Weight	125kg (19st)
Chest	116cm (46in)
Hips	125cm (49in)
Boots	13

DEBUT	26-6-94 v. France, Christchurch

All Blacks Points	200 (40 tries)
All Blacks games	65
First class games	164
First class points	560 (112 tries)

In the 1995 World Cup he was the first All Blacks since 1905 to score four tries in a test against England.

He set World Cup records by scoring:
- 15 tries in the tournament,
- eight tries in the 1999 series,
- tries in five consecutive games.

Besides being the youngest ever All Blacks he is world's youngest player to score 10 Test tries and the first player to score 12 test tries in a calendar year.

REPRESENTED

New Zealand Under 17 1991-92
New Zealand Secondary schools 1992-93

Test Record: (+) *stands for substitute and* (-) *means replaced*

1994	France, Christchurch, 8-22; France, Auckland. 20-23.
1995	Ireland (World Cup), Johannesburg, 43-19 (two tries); Wales, Johannesburg, 34-9 (-); Scotland, quarter-final, Pretoria, 48-30 (one try); England, semi-final, Cape Town, 45-29 (four tries); South Africa, final, Johannesburg, 12-15; Australia, Auckland, 28-16 (one try); Australia, Sydney, 34-23 (one try); Italy, Bologna, 70-6 (one try); France, Toulouse, 15-22; France, Paris, 37-12 (one try).
1996	Samoa, Napier, 51-10; Scotland, Dunedin, 62-31 (one try) (-); Australia,Wellington, 43-6 (one try); South Africa, Christchurch, 15-11; Australia, Brisbane, 32-25.
1997	England, Manchester, 25-8; Wales, London, 42-7; England, London, 26-26.

1998	England, Dunedin, 64-22 (one try); England, Auckland, 40-10 (-); Australia, Melbourne, 16-24 (+); South Africa, Wellington, 3-13; Australia, Christchurch, 23-27 (one try); South Africa, Durban, 23-24; Australia, Sydney 14-19.
1999	Samoa, Albany 71-13 (one try) (+); South Africa, Dunedin, 28-0 (+); Australia, Auckland, 34-15 (+); South Africa, Pretoria, 34-18 (+); Australia, Sydney, 7-28 (+); Tonga, WorldCup, Bristol, 45-9 (two tries); England, London, 30-16 (one try); Italy, Huddersfield, 101-3 (two tries); Scotland, Edinburgh, 30-18; France, semi-final, London, 31-43 (two tries); South Africa, playoff, Cardiff, 18-22.
2000	Tonga, Albany, 102-0; Scotland, Dunedin, 69-20 (three tries); Scotland, Auckland, 48-14; Australia, Sydney, 39-35 (one try); South Africa, Christchurch, 25-12; Australia, Wellington, 23-24; South Africa, Johannesburg, 40-46; France, Paris, 39-26.

2001   Argentina, Christchurch, 67-19;
France, Wellington, 37-12 (one try);
South Africa, Cape Town, 12-3;
Australia, Dunedin, 15-23 (one try);
South Africa, Auckland, 26-15;
Australia, Sydney 26-29; Ireland,
Dublin, 40-29 (one try); Scotland,
Edinburgh 37-6 (one try);
Argentina, Buenos Aires, 24-20
(one try).

TEST RECORD

Country	P	W	D	L	t	pts
Argentina	2	2	-	-	1	5
Australia	13	6	-	7	6	30
England	6	5	1	-	6	30
France	7	3	-	4	4	20
Ireland	2	2	-	-	3	15
Italy	2	2	-	-	4	20
Samoa	2	2	-	-	1	5
Scotland	6	6	-	-	7	35
South Africa	11	6	-	5	-	-
Tonga	2	2	-	-	2	10
Wales	2	2	-	-	-	-
TOTAL	55	38	1	16	34	170

The Author

KEVIN CHILDS IS a lifelong follower of rugby. He reported on the game in New Zealand. Since then he has been a journalist on ten newspapers in three countries. Kevin has contributed to the New York Times and the International Edition of the London Guardian, is the author of six books, lectures in journalism and is a media consultant.

Other *Legend* books

Karrie Webb
By Charles Happell

Gilly
The Story of Adam Gilchrist
By Garrie Hutchinson

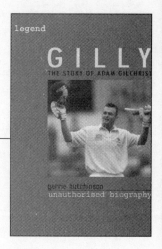

Kostya Tzsyu
By Dominic Cadden